center

A system of six practices
for pursuing your
passions and purposes
in self, family, work,
and community.

Darrell Velegol

Wild Scholars Media

CENTER

A system of six practices for taking charge of your passions and purposes in self, family, work, and community.

Copyright © 2013 by Darrell Velegol.

ISBN-13: 978-1491094624
ISBN-10: 1491094621

This book is written in 10 pt Times New Roman font.
Cover by Andy Mylin (www.AndyMylin.com)

For information about workshops or seminars, or to send comments, suggestions, or corrections, please email CENTERpractices@gmail.com.

Darrell Velegol
2013 August 29 (for Fall 2013)

Dedicated to my loving, wise, and beautiful wife
Dr. Stephanie Butler Velegol,
whose ideas and encouragement give breath to this venture.

Brief Contents

Detailed Contents

Preface

*Far away there in the sunshine are my
highest aspirations. I may not reach them,
but I can look up and see their beauty,
believe in them, and try to follow where they
lead. – Louisa May Alcott*

*Learning is any change in a system that
produces a more or less permanent change in
its capacity for adapting to its environment. –
Herbert A. Simon*

In my position as a professor at Penn State, I have spoken with
hundreds of students and professionals who want answers to
questions like, "What is the key to becoming a great leader in my
field?" "How can I do what I *really* love to do, in my career and in
my community?" "How do I balance family and work?" My
response has evolved over time. In my first few years, I had all the
answers for them. "Just listen to this bit of wisdom dripping off my
lips." But with experience, I have come to see that each of us is
called to a different purpose, and each has different passions.

Before I understood this fully, I would bring into my classes at
Penn State well-known quotations, from people like Ben Franklin,
Mother Teresa, Harriet Beecher Stowe, or Winston Churchill. At
first, I used them primarily to break up my class time, adding a bit
of life to lectures that were filled with equations and diagrams.

After I while, I started listening to the words that I myself was
quoting! One person would talk about sticking to the work, and I
would think, "Yes! That's the secret! Stick with it!" And another

would talk about the importance of having a good team around you, and I would think, "Yes! That's the secret! Join or build a strong team!" And another would talk about the importance of having deeply held beliefs, and I would think, "Yes! I just need to find and shape what I believe, and hold firm to that!" But who was right? What is the secret of being successful? And what is "success" anyway? There were too many maxims, too many quotations, too many exhortations. I found myself a bit lost.

In 2007 I had a sabbatical. During the course of that year, the various pieces started coming together, and I realized that there was truth in each of the various approaches suggested by these famous quotes and stories. I came to realize that success was not limited to those having the title of President, Olympic gold medalist, Nobel Prize winner, CEO, millionaire. As the famous UCLA basketball coach John Wooden stated in his "Pyramid of Success",[1] "Success is peace of mind which is a direct result of self-satisfaction in knowing you made the effort to become the best of which you are capable." Success is measured by the effort we pour into those activities we love, more than by worldly medals and trophies.

When I returned to the classroom in Spring 2008, I started giving not only 15 second quotes, but 1-minute stories about successful people. I included "regular folks" – great people such as my Dad or my grandmother. Over several years, my stories took the shape of a set of practices, which can be summarized by the acronym *CENTER*, which stands for:

Character
Entrepreneurship
owNership
Tenacity
Excellence
Relationship

These days, a number of my students tell me that learning the CENTER practices has been more important for their careers than the technical information they learned in my courses, such as thermodynamics or heat transfer. The CENTER practices have enabled many students to utilize what they had learned in the classroom in professional settings, as well as in family and community life. The practices are not new; rather, they are practices that originated with hundreds of others. I have continued to learn from my students probably more than they have learned from me! If I have any contribution, it is in reading many books and research articles, observing many people and organizations, and in systemizing the practices into a coherent whole.

This book is my first attempt to put the CENTER practices into a coherent whole. I see this book as a long term effort, with periodic improvements coming, and I hope that you will help me to improve this material over time, by emailing suggestions or corrections.

My aim in this book is to provide a system that you can use in life, whether you are in middle school, or college, or 40 years old, or 75 years old. The system consists of 36 skills that make up the CENTER practices. As the quote at the beginning of this Preface says, I hope that you can learn and adapt this system to increase your own capacity to accomplish your great passions and purposes.

Darrell Velegol
State College, Pennsylvania
2013 August 29
CENTERpractices@gmail.com

center

A system of six practices
for pursuing your
passions and purposes
in self, family, work,
and community.

Darrell Velegol

CENTER – an Overview

The whole is greater than the sum of the parts. –
Aristotle, Metaphysics, Book 8[2]

Pursuing dreams. Sebastian's story.

At first I paused only slightly at my friend Sebastian's declaration: "Darrell, I'm thinking of changing careers." At the time – the late 1990s – Sebastian and I were lab mates at Carnegie Mellon University, both pursuing graduate degrees in Chemical Engineering. His Romanian accent seemed to add emphasis to his words. With a slight raising of my eyebrows, I invited him to continue. "I want to become a professional opera singer."

By this point in our friendship, I knew that Sebastian loved opera. During one weekend when he was set to travel, he lamented that he would be missing the weekend production of Puccini's opera *Tosca*. "What do you mean 'missing it'? Do you have a ticket for the show?" "No, no, no. The Metropolitan Opera in New York broadcasts their Saturday opera each week by radio, and this week is *Tosca*. It's a very good opera. Very good." So that Saturday afternoon, I found the radio channel for the broadcast, and set my audio tape deck to record it. The performance to me was simply a group of people singing loudly in a language I did not understand. I could discern nothing more.

When I brought the cassette on Monday, Sebastian was elated! He thanked me, and gladly accepted the small gift. But on Tuesday, he entered the lab and asked, "Darrell, where are the other two acts of Tosca?" I had not realized that operas are performed in multiple acts. And so when the first act ended, I stopped the recording.

Sebastian looked at me for a second, and then broke into his resonant baritone laugh. "OK, Darrell, so let me tell you about *Tosca* ...." "And then the villain Scarpia sings Va Tosca. And the chimes are ringing, and the violins are whining." At this point, Sebastian sang part of the aria, "Va, Tosca ..." "And then Scarpia closes the aria with, 'Tosca, mi fai dimenticare Iddio.' 'Tosca, you make me forget God.' Can you believe he said that?"

I was spellbound, almost breathless. Sebastian had brought the story to life. And I understood my friend in a new way. He felt about opera, like I felt about Chemical Engineering. Opera was not merely something that he would do for his career; rather, opera was part of who Sebastian is, part of his **Character**.

And yet, I wondered ... How would he become an opera singer? How would he know where to start? How would he support himself? What if it did not work out? He was already 26 years old – was it too late for him to start? Who would help him? So how did opera become part of Sebastian's Character, and how would he go from this Character, to singing on the stage of the Metropolitan Opera House and other great opera houses all over the world? How does each person find the few things he or she is most passionate about, move through the countless steps – and perhaps even more missteps – to move forward, and bring about deep and lasting change in his or her own life? And ... the lives of those nearby? Answering that question is the subject of this book.

Three villains that thwart our dreams.

In pursuing our dreams, like Sebastian did, there are many challenges. However, three particular problems – I call them "villains" – arise again and again. In 1000 different guises, the #1 villain ... is fear. Fear of losing your job. Fear of flunking the test. Fear of losing the girl. Fear of looking stupid. Fear of hearing no. Fear of losing later opportunities. Fear of being a victim of a crime.

There is no end to the fears we encounter. As the well-known acronym says, FEAR = false evidence appearing real. Of course, sometimes fear has a truthful basis. However, it is seldom the whole story. Behind every fear, there is often some good thing that we throw away, because of a small probability event that we fear. Fear is the #1 villain. How does a person overcome fear? It is not easy. It involves issues with Character (see the exercise on "Courage Mirror") and Tenacity (see the exercises on "Voices", "Battle Plan", and "Transitions".)

A second villain is lack of focus. Certainly in my own life, I struggle with having too many "priorities", too many emails, too many meetings, too many deadlines, too many bills, too many books to read. I love the horse riding scene in the movie *City Slickers*. Mitch Robbins, the 39 year old New Yorker played by Billy Crystal, and Curly, the experienced cowboy played by Jack Palance, have the following exchange[3]:

CURLY: You know what the secret o' life is?
MITCH: No. What?
CURLY: This. [Holding up one finger.]
MITCH: Your finger?
CURLY: One thing. Just one thing. You stick to that and everything else don't mean shiiit.
MITCH: That's great, but what's the one thing?
CURLY: That's what you've gotta figure out.

What is your "one thing"? OK, maybe you might have a couple "one things". But if you find yourself having 25 "one things", then I suspect you are as confused as Mitch Robbins is in the movie. How does a person gain focus? You might try looking at your Character (see the exercise on "Life Ring") and owNership (see the exercises on "Flood Choices" and "Big Rock Choices").

Another villain is the inability to conduct experiments in life – to try things – either due to excessive certainty about the result, or due to excessive doubt, or due to pride that "I should just know this". I believe in trying small experiments – early, fast, cheap, frequent – for all aspects of my life. I call them "1% experiments", since they often take 1% of a year, or about 88 hours. Some experiments I try a few times, just to make sure. But once I become convinced that some skill or practice works in my life, I find a way to incorporate it broadly. Conversely, when I find a practice that decreases my ability to pursue my "one thing(s)", I find a way to drop it. Those 1% experiments are essential to learning and mapping my way.

CENTER. A system of practices for pursuing dreams.

On the one hand, a person might think that experience is the key, that as one experiences more of life, that the strategies for moving forward will be automatically learned. The challenge is that there are too many possibilities in life! If we had to make every mistake that could be made, in order to move forward, we would run out of time! We need to "model our life" using a consistent method.

One model for making the leap toward a successful life, as defined by how well we pursue our purposes, is to work through the practices of *CENTER*. CENTER is an acronym, that stands for

Character
Entrepreneurship
owNership
Tenacity
Excellence
Relationship

Below I summarize a somewhat deeper meaning for the words. In the next section we will see how Sebastian worked through each of these pieces. What we find is not simply a summation of six different practices, but an overall emergent behavior, such that when all six combine, they breathe life into an entirely new way of thinking, comprehensive in its scope.

<u>C</u>*haracter. The key blanks to fill in are ... I am _____; I will be _____.*

Various people might write: I am a teacher. I am creative. I am a coal miner. I am a person of deep faith. I am a champion for literacy. I am the voice of the trees. I am heterosexual ... or gay. I am sober. I will be sober. I will be a giver. I will be a surgeon. I will be a mother. Some people might write: I do not know who I am. I do not know what I will be. I have tried to be _____, but it did not work.

<u>E</u>*ntrepreneurship. The key blank to fill in is ... I run smart experiments and take smart risks toward my dream of _____.*
Various people might write I run experiments and risks toward my dream of: starting my own business, changing my family dinner hour, composing country music, winning an election, serving on city council, being a published author. Some people might write: I am not running any useful experiments or taking any significant risks. Others might write: I took some significant risks, and got burned. Still others might write: When I work on my dream of being a prominent chef, it is almost like *play*!

ow<u>N</u>ership. The key blank to fill in is ... Based on my Character, I choose _____, and then permit my agency to hustle, execute, and systemize my choices.
Various people might write: I choose to have a healthy and energetic body. I choose to save 10% of my income. I choose to have a 2-hour date each week with my spouse. I choose to drink just one

glass of wine each evening. I choose to sleep 7 hours per night. I choose to be 10 minutes early for appointments. Others might write: I do not state any choices; my life is chaos. Still others might write: I do not have any choices; I feel controlled by other people, or outside events.

Tenacity. *The key blank to fill in is … I will hold on in pursuing my vision of _____, amidst all obstacles.*
Various people might write I will hold on in my pursuit toward: finishing my college degree, staying happily married, staying married, losing 50 pounds, winning the tennis championship, getting my green card. Others might write I will hold on in my pursuit toward: getting my PhD, as long as I learn one new thing each week; running the Boston Marathon, as long as I am able to move; fighting for Civil Rights, until I am gone.

Excellence. *The key blank to fill in is … I commit and focus hard work on gaining skill in _____.*
Various people might write I plan and focus hard work on gaining skill in: playing piano, working in teams, solving differential equations, jazz dance, being a dad, painting artistic works. Others might write: I am not good at anything. I work on playing guitar, but I'm just dabbling.

Relationship. *The key blanks to fill in are …My family is _____; my home is _____.*
Various people might write: My family includes my wife and two children. My family includes the people on my church council. My family includes my business co-founders. My family includes my roommates. My home is Centre City Philadelphia. My home is Penn State. Others might write: I am lonely. I don't know where is my home. I don't feel like anyone likes me.

Together, these six practices form the acronym **CENTER**.[4] Filling in those blanks takes a lot of effort and thought, and often requires that we run many experiments in life. This book provides exercises and measures for guiding you to fill in the blanks of CENTER. By writing words like those listed, you will identify where you want to go, and begin charting a path toward that vision.

Some books are focused on one aspect, but ignore the system. CENTER provides a "life system" framework, enabling us to make choices that help our entire life to move forward. This does not mean that the six practices will make us "well-rounded" in the usual sense of knowing a little math, a little literature, a little history, a little of everything. "Well-rounded" can be code for "mediocre". Rather, using CENTER is like keeping a healthy body, not just a healthy leg or arm or eyes or heart. Let us examine a diagram, which shows some of the relationships of the CENTER practices.

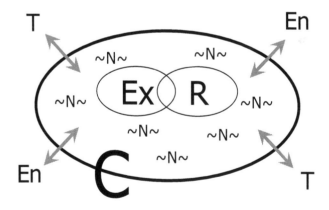

Character defines everything that goes into and comes out of a person. Character (C) is "who I am". Within that boundary, I determine how I will balance the tasks I will do and the people I will interact with. For tasks, I want to pursue Excellence (Ex); for people, I want to pursue Relationship (R). Relationships are not something "out there", but are in the core of a person. For example, when my children are ill, I feel ill – they are a part of me. CENTER sees tasks and relationships both in tension, and in synergy.

The tasks and the relationships swim in the protoplasm of life, which CENTER calls "owNership". Yes, the "N" is the third letter of the word owNership … after all, it was Francis Bacon who told us, "There is no excellent beauty that hath not some strangeness in the proportion." ☺   owNership provides the logistical and tactical details of life, of how you will make choices about your time, energy, money, and similar resources.

External to ourselves, we often have disturbances or attacks on our lives, and we must have the Tenacity (T) to ward those off. Otherwise, they might harm our pursuit. At the same time, there are external opportunities and aspirations, and we must take risks in trying to harness those through Entrepreneurship (En).

Sebastian and CENTER.

How did Sebastian move through the CENTER practices? Sebastian's Character had been formed since he was a boy. It turns out that both his Dad and his Mom were well-known professional opera singers in Romania. Many nights, young Sebastian would go to the theatre and see one or both of his parents perform. At home, he watched them practice their arias; he watched them listen to previous performances; he watched himself internalize the stories and the music. That love of opera and the theatre were scratched into his Character.

Sebastian grew up in Nicolae Ceauşescu's Romania. Conditions were harsh. And so his parents set to leave in 1989. Right before the move, Sebastian's father died, and the family almost did not leave. After a helpful warning from a friend and some rapid action, they did depart Romania, to live near Detroit,

Michigan. Sebastian learned that he could make major life changes, experiment with life, and take significant risks, and still be OK. He did this later when he asked for an audition with a well-known musician at Carnegie Mellon University.

After Sebastian decided to pursue an opera career, he still had bills to pay. He still had to live. He got a part time job as a lab technician – cleaning beakers and doing other small labor – in the Department of Chemical Engineering. He coordinated his singing lessons at Duquesne University and practice schedule with Claudia Pinza, the daughter of the famous bass singer Ezio Pinza, and he worked a part-time job at CMU in the Department of Chemical Engineering. That is, he took owNership of his life, full responsibility.

Numerous events were difficult for Sebastian during the process. He got discouraging comments from various quarters. He was still working to finish his Masters Degree, as he had promised to do. There were times he was overwhelmed, and times that life was full of drudgery. Sebastian had built mechanisms around himself, to ward off the voices and continue through. He watched hockey and football. He continued to see friends. He set a finish date for his Masters Degree in Chemical Engineering. And he enrolled in a 2-year music program, in order to keep him moving forward.

Excellence came with time for Sebastian, and having the degree program, with Claudia Pinza as his teacher – was very important. Those two years, plus summers spent with Mrs. Pinza in Italy, were instrumental in helping him go from someone with a great raw talent, to someone who could add the right color, intonation, and depth to his voice.

For relationships, Sebastian had a firm grasp of who was his family, and where was his home. He had his mother – his amazing mother – who continued to encourage him. This is a luxury that many people do not have. Sebastian also gave time and laughter to many friends, and they became part of his family. For his home, Sebastian stayed in Pittsburgh, where he still lives today.

From your experiences to your future, with integrity.

In using CENTER, the aim is not to learn how to become more busy, nor to start from scratch. Rather, you will start from your own experiences in life. By synergizing the structure and perspective of CENTER with your own experiences, you will start to work toward those things that you are passionate about, which capture your own heart, and you'll improve your integrity, which is having consistency in all parts of your life.

Some of you will read these words about CENTER, and how these practices can lead you toward pursuing your purposes, but you do not believe that this could really happen to you. But yes, I am writing for YOU. These words are coming not from some expert at a university, as much as from a fellow experimenter in life, who has had many, many failures, and some measure of successes, by my own standards.

And so now it is your turn. Before we look more deeply at the CENTER practices, take one hour to fill in the blanks for yourself. Give yourself permission[5] to experiment with various words. For now, allow yourself to write things that might startle or offend others who know you; you can just keep your words private.   This document is not the final version, but the first of many experiments in this book. The most important place to start, is by establishing those things that are part of your Character, and finding which parts you choose to change. That is the subject of the next chapter.

Action Checklist

☐ **CENTER blanks.** Fill the blanks listed earlier (given again below), in 60 minutes or less. The idea is to consider the ideas early on, before reading the rest of this book.

☐ **Daily review.** Take 5-10 minutes each day to reflect on your Life Ring. Over time, you will likely see inconsistencies, which you can resolve – or life will reveal! – to improve your integrity.[6] Integrity is about having self-consistent beliefs. The daily review will also help you avoid unnecessary hurry.

Character. I am _____; I will be _____.

Entrepreneurship. I run smart experiments and take smart risks toward my dream of _____.

owNership. Based on my Character, I choose _____, and then permit my agency to hustle, execute, and systemize my choices.

Tenacity. I will hold on in pursuing my vision of _____, amidst all obstacles.

Excellence. I commit and focus hard work on gaining skill in _____.

Relationship. My family is _____; my home is _____.

Here are some suggested additional books to read. These appear on "Velegol's top shelf".

- Dale Carnegie, *How to Win Friends and Influence People.*
- Stephen Covey, *7 Habits of Highly Effective People.*
- Timothy Ferriss, *The 4-Hour Workweek.*
- Michael Gerber. *The E-Myth Revisited.*
- Jack Matson, *Innovate or Die.*

Character

Character. I am _____ ; I will be _____ .

Χαρακτήρας (kharaktēr) is the Greek word providing the origin for the English word "Character". Kharaktēr in turn comes from Greek words meaning "to inscribe", or "pointed stick". The etymology is significant. Character, which is the set of qualities or distinctive traits that distinguishes a person, comes from moments when Life has used a sharp stick to inscribe or scratch into your heart and mind. The memories from these scratches are usually poignant, soaked with great meaning, and often providing identity. And oftentimes, these scratches provide the *courage* to surge forward.

When I turned 30 years old, I feel in hindsight that I had only some character. I use the word "some" rather than "good" or "bad", because when I was 30 years old, I my wife and my faith were deeply important to me, and I loved what I was good at – Chemical Engineering – but I did not yet feel a compelling sense of "Yes! I will sacrifice deeply for my purpose in …". There were few people or tasks that had my unrestrained affection and love.

Having a large and strong character – one that has deeply held convictions about justice, business, community, marriage, and other aspects of life – is a common trait that I see among my own heroes. It gives them their courage, enabling them to keep their vision above their own self. George Washington believed that "Good moral character is the first essential in a man." When I look at Washington, or Mother Teresa, or Gandhi, or Eleanor Roosevelt, I see people of towering character, with unshakeable convictions and courage. When I look at scientists I admire, such as Nobel Prize winner Herb Simon, or social entrepreneurs I admire, such as Nobel Prize winner Muhammad Yunus, I see persons of deep character.

Developing a strong character usually takes many years of experience to develop and refine and shape. Through our years of experience, we come to say – sometimes proudly, sometimes not – "I am ..." white, black, Sunni, smart, born again, beautiful, a drug addict, a leader, slow, a family man, a business woman, creative, a dancer, or another label. Sometimes we like our identities, and sometimes not.

Victor Frankl discovered that between the stimuli that happen to us, and our response, is a space. That space is defined and bounded by our character. What will you aim to put in that gap? Do we really have the power to modify or revolutionize our Character? Can we have a Character that yields courage and hope during trials, rather than cowardice and fear? Here we will explore five skills that will help reveal, define, and shape our Character.

Your character might or might not match your career. If you want to be the best in your chosen career, your character might need to include your career; however, for many, their careers provides the resources – for example in money, connections, resources – that enable their true calling.

1 Scratch List. Focus past events to urgent passions.

Within 3 miles of where my wife Stephanie grew up, in Moorestown, Jersey, a young girl was born and raised named Alice Paul.[8] William Paul was a successful businessman, and he and his wife Tacie raised their daughter Alice with strong Quaker values – which then as now, includes gender equality.[9] Tacie was a member of the National American Woman Suffrage Association (NAWSA), which became the modern day League of Women Voters.[10] Alice was often with Tacie at the NAWSA meetings.

Alice was a bright student, graduating first in her Friends School class in 1901. Friends Schools have Quaker origins, and numerous champions for women's suffrage were Quakers, including Susan B. Anthony and Lucretia Mott. Alice went on to Swarthmore College, which promoted a Quaker-inspired education, and she earned a degree in biology. The college yearbook called Alice, "An open-hearted maiden, pure and true."

In 1907 came a turning point. Alice visited Birmingham, England, in order to study social work. It was there that she met Christabel Pankhurst, a leader of the Women's Social and Political Union (WSPU) in Britain. The WSPU did not shy away from more aggressive tactics, and Alice was arrested and jailed numerous times, including for smashing windows to gain publicity for the suffrage movement.

After returning to the United States, Alice Paul and others formed the National Woman's Party. The NWP was very active, but did not use the militant tactics that Alice had learned in the WSPU. The NWP picketed the White House of President Woodrow Wilson, one of the first large-scale examples of the use of non-violent protest in the United States. Eventually, Alice and her followers were physically attacked, jailed in rat-infested cells, and force-fed after they engaged a hunger strike.

Eventually the treatment of the suffragists became publicly known. Shortly thereafter, President Wilson declared that women's suffrage was a "war time necessity", and the 19th Amendment, drafted by Susan B. Anthony, started movement passage and ratification.[11] The story is told powerfully in the 2004 HBO movie *Iron Jawed Angels*, starring Hillary Swank.

How did Alice Paul become a central player in the women's suffrage movement? We can start to answer this, by examining her

"Scratch List". She grew up in a Quaker home, with a mother dedicated to the cause of women's suffrage. She no doubt heard women in her house lamenting their lack of having the vote. Scratch. Alice then went to Swarthmore, where she met a number of faculty and others who believed in social change. Scratch. After that, Alice went to England, where she worked with more aggressive suffragists. Scratch. There were likely numerous other scratches that made Alice Paul who she was – the pattern is there.

What is your Scratch List? Aristotle said, "We cannot learn without pain." Most scratches hurt – the events might be moments of significant brokenness – although a few scratches might be wonderfully joyful events. Perhaps you are a person who was scratched by one or more of the following types of events:

- a boy, whose parents got a divorce
- an employee, who had a stinging interchange with the boss
- a student, so-so who got mostly C's, or perhaps an A student who got a painful B
- a young man, whose wedding engagement was broken
- a widow, who lost her husband young
- a mother, whose daughter had a life-threatening illness
- a middle-aged worker, who had a heart attack.
- a daughter, who watched her diligent single mother take care of the family for 20 years
- a husband, whose wife spent late nights earning a college degree
- a child, who was emotionally or physically abused
- a PhD student, who won a prestigious award
- an addict – of alcohol, drugs, gambling, pornography – who has tremendous guilt or shame
- a professional, who desperately craved the approval of a boss or clients … and didn't get it

As we will see, the Scratch List is only the beginning of defining our Character. Popeye the Sailorman famously said, "I yam what I yam and tha's all what I yam." But we are not cartoon characters. Our Scratch List tells us what we have been through, and suggests what might be of central importance to us, but that list need not become our identity. We might have been divorced; we might have owned a business that failed; we might have had cancer. Those are scratching events we might have been through, in difficult tests of life. But these events do not have to be who "we are". In examining the next two skills, "Life Ring" and "Courage Mirror", we will see that we can use those scratches to energize and change who we are. Or as Victor Frankl said, we have the power to choose.

Exercise 1. Write down your Scratch List.

Include perhaps 3 or 5 or 10 events in your life (or your organization) that fundamentally changed who you are today. You might work on this exercise solo, or with a partner or group who knows you well. It is important to write down your Scratch List, because the power of written words is significant. For each scratch write if you are hopeful about the future, or fearful. Hope looks toward a positive outcome, while fear comes from shame, embarrassment, disgust, dread, self doubt, and similar concepts.

The purpose of this exercise is to identify poignant events in your past, which might energize areas of passion to pursue in your future. Those areas of our life, or our organizations, that were the most biting in the past – trials, adversities, losses – are often areas that we are uniquely equipped to tackle in the future.

2 Life Ring. Focus your present with integrity.

When I first met my good friend Brian Cunningham, a highly accomplished entrepreneur who lives near Washington DC, he said,

"Darrell, let me show you who I am." He proceeded to pull out a laminated sheet – just one sheet of paper – that had a red square in the center of the page – his overall "life goal" – with a number of blue ovals around the center and connected to it. In 15 minutes, he was able to summarize his current life, including his wife, his children and grandchildren, his businesses, his community outreach program, his Bible study, and other areas. He closed with, "Now tell me about yourself." I was left just a bit speechless …

The beauty of that document, which I have come to call a "Life Ring", is that it focused his energies into just a few areas, and it puts them in one place. Summarizing your arenas on one sheet also can improve your integrity, which is often sacrificed when we try to keep track of too many things. I have given a template for a Life Ring under the Life Ring exercise in a couple pages. Brian avoided the hundreds of distractions that might entangle us. Focus-focus-focus! Dropping the "good" things in life, enables us to choose the "best" things. In my own life, I used to watch a number of political shows, feeling, "It behooves someone like me to be a well-informed citizen." In actuality, I gained little from those shows, and they wasted one to two hours each evening. I now recognize that there are better ways for me to be informed, and to use that time better.

Of great significance to Brian's life ring was the middle of it: "A life that's fun, interesting, and purpose driven." That guided everything else in his Life Ring. What is the driving force[12] in your life? Your wife? Your kids? Your boss? Posterity? Science? Security and money? Fear? Political party? Principles? Lust? Alcohol or drugs? Friends? Health? Efficiency? Hurts from yesterday or hopes for tomorrow? Principles? Whatever you consider to be the driving force in your life, or by what you measure the meaning in your life, goes in the middle of the Life Ring – the "master in the middle".

Some might declare, "My spouse is important in everything I do, and so I don't want to make her just one bubble on the ring." I understand. That said, Mr. Cunningham's approach has a power behind it, in that since my spouse is on my Life Ring, I am intentional about scheduling weekly dates with her, prioritizing her wishes, and finding ways to grow our relationship. Any item in which I dedicate time, is on my Life Ring.

When I made my first draft of my Life Ring, I had more than 25 ovals on it! I came to realize that I was trying to make everything a priority, like bolding every letter in a book. Trying to do too many items, splintering our time and energy into too many bins, is what I see from most of the students and professionals with whom I interact. Who doesn't have too many things to do?

In my own case, with time I made the hard decisions to stop doing certain items at work, halt leadership roles in some organizations I was part of, and decline various invitations and offers. I made the decision to say a "big YES" to those few items in which I would invest most heavily. I pruned the Life Ring. My effort in life is higher than it has ever been, and now that the effort is focused on roughly one third the items, my impact has increased.

Under each oval heading, add some of the habits you intend for that arena.[13] There is not enough room to list 1000 habits, on one page. And so list those top few habits in each bubble, where you will commit to spend time each day or each week. Let the others fade. Part of the wisdom in sticking with the 1-page Life Ring is that each morning, I can review it and refocus. Because I am able to fit only 3 or 4 short bullets under each heading in the Life Ring, I must choose what to do, and what to exclude, in clear ways.

You might have far too many items, which can leave you confused about direction, or conversely, you might have too few items, which can be so vague that they are not actionable. Each day, review your Life Ring, and edit and update as often as you see necessary. Drafting a Life Ring can take hours, but in my own case, it has taken years to get it to a state where I feel that my life is focused somewhat. I am confident there is much further to go.

In the first Chapter, I mentioned that the #1 villain is fear, and #2 is lack of focus. Drawing and continually asserting a Life Ring is a powerful way to focus. Follow Miller's "magic number 7, plus or minus 2", having 5 to 9 major arenas, each summarized in a bubble around the master in the middle, and then add a few sub-bullets, that still fit on 1 page.

Our character guides how we proactively initiate thoughts and actions – especially guiding how we choose to live in the next hour – as well as how we reactively respond to the events of life that happen to us. Of the letters in CENTER, "C" is the most significant, because of its strategic role in guiding all the other letters. By studying the lives of many leaders I admire in science, engineering, music, politics, sports, business, and other fields, I see that much of their effort has been in developing the "C", and once it is formed, they can ENTER the rest of their lives to achieve a great purpose. In contrast, some people live lives showing amazing talent or skill, but if they lack a driving force in their Character, they often receive little satisfaction from their efforts. The driving force thus describes a type of life calling.

Knowing one's character enables us to be strategic about every decision in our lives; in later chapters of this book, we will see that owNership then enables us to apply the tactics and logistics to help us attain our strategic steps, hour by hour.

Exercise 2. Draw your Life Ring.

I have given a template at the end of this exercise. Start by giving a photo or schematic of your "master in the middle"; this is the primary driving force behind all your decisions – and in every life, there can only be one master[14]. If you try to have more than one master, eventually your Life will intersect events so that you have an "identity quake"[15], and must choose your primary master.[16] Then focus on roughly 5-9 major life arenas where you will invest your time, with self, family, work, and community (SFWC). Within each arena, list those most important habits that you will commit to each day or each week. This is not simply a "to do list", but a list of habits. When the Life Ring has a clear "master in the middle", 5-9 arenas, and a short list of habits under each arena, it is complete, and will help your integrity.

Life Ring Template

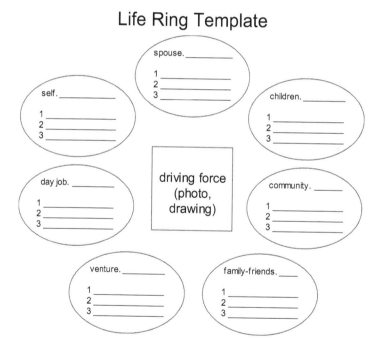

3 Courage Mirror. Design the future you.

In my freshman year in high school, there was a girl I had a crush on. We were sitting together at a high school assembly, when one of the football players turned around and made a joke about us. We were both enormously embarrassed, and the girl hardly spoke with me again. At the time, I was about 6 feet tall, but I was very skinny. It was the classic "Charles Atlas" moment, when the boy gets sand kicked in his face, and decides to gain some muscle. It didn't take long for me to fixate on a hero for that part of my life: Arnold Schwarzenegger. I read books – *Arnold: The Education of a Bodybuilder* had the most grand bicep photo I had seen[17,18] – watched the movie *Pumping Iron* literally hundreds of times, got posters, and even went to a Mr. Olympia show. I decided that I wanted to have a different look, and I visualized it continuously.[19]

Within a couple years, the results were noticeable. My muscles were better defined, and I at least wasn't getting sand kicked in my face anymore. By the time I was a senior, I was at the top of the heap in terms of weightlifting for my high school. I just kept letting Arnold Schwarzenegger talk to me, telling me who I wanted to authentically wanted to be, pouring courage into my heart. He formed part of my "Courage Mirror", which I sometimes also call my "Power Mirror".

Who do you want to be? Perhaps you stumble across a grand vision, and you just cannot let it go, like Robert H. Goddard and his "cherry tree dream".[20] Perhaps you just visited the doctor, and he or she had some alarming news, and you will need to change your diet significantly. Or perhaps you have made mistakes, maybe big mistakes, and for one reason or another, you might not be "enough". Are the voices whispering to you, "You're not smart enough, fast enough, beautiful enough, personable enough, rich enough, educated enough …" Perhaps the voices you hear … are yours? Don't let the past steal your future. As Benjamin Franklin once said,

"There are croakers in every country, always boding its ruin."[21] Beware the croakers. You might not be able to change everything, but most likely, you can change significantly.

By placing your Courage Mirror around your home or apartment, you can have the walls and rooms speak to your heart day after day, minute after minute, who you will be. The theory of visualization is well established in the sports literature, as well as other literature,[22] and "learned helplessness" and "learned confidence" have been studied extensively.[23] What paintings will you display, what music will you listen to, what type of furniture will you use, whose photos will you hang, what scents will you let linger? You can control all of these sensory inputs in your living space, and often in your office space. Where will you travel? What courses will you take? What TV shows will you watch? Create a Courage Mirror that lifts you up, encourages you, rather than reminds you of failures or negative experiences, or that discourage you.

Whatever you place in the blanks "I am _____; I will be _____," will pursue after you. If you say, "I am a C student," and leave it there, C's will follow you. If you say, "I do good work, and get paid a decent wage," a decent wage will follow you. If you say, "I will always be poor," poverty will follow you. If you say, "I do great work, and I will be a leader in this field, and I will receive significant compensation," that is what will tend to pursue you. You are inviting the filled blanks into your life. If you invite negative "I am's", they will spread like bamboo in your life.

In the Velegol home, we have paintings of Washington Crossing the Delaware, to inspire us toward Tenacity. We have professionally-done photos of our family having fun, reminding us of the joy in our Relationships. We have a painting from a local artist, which we purchased at a silent auction at our local Montessori school, reminding us of the importance of a discovery-based education. We have da Vinci's Last Supper hanging over our dining room table, as a reminder of our faith, and of a wonderful meal. We have books on our shelves by Stephen Covey and Dale Carnegie, and about Martin Luther King Jr. and Mother Teresa. Who are your heroes? Who do you want to be? See big, and expect greatness to pursue you.[24]

You might be thinking, "I don't want to be phony and try to be like other people. I want to be *me*." I agree. You are aiming to be the best, authentic *you* that you can be. The Courage Mirror aims to do just that. You are not trying to become another person, but you very much might want to imitate some aspect of a person. You might want to imitate some of Arnold Schwarzenegger's bodybuilding skills, Maya Angelou's oratory skills[25], or Oprah Winfrey's interviewing skills. You want to imitate aspects of those you admire – learning from them – as if they are your mentors, even while you want to be yourself. Will you risk imitating aspects of those heroes you admire, running some personal experiments, so that you can become the best you possible?

If you feel empty of Character, this is a great time to run some experiments. If you are unsure of whether a certain poster will speak to you, run the experiment! Put up a poster – perhaps without a frame at first – and see if it fades out of your mind, or if every time you look at it, you feel energized. Book travel to someplace that you think might inspire you – you won't know until you go.[26] Our instincts are often shaped by powerful experiments or experiences we undertake, sometimes of our own choosing. If we haven't run enough experiments in life, it is time to start! Run experiments that will jolt and build your Character, and allow the time – sometimes years – for your Character and identity to incubate and grow.[27]

I want my decisions being guided by voices that I have deliberately chosen, in moments of relative sanity. There are more than enough discouraging voices in the world – we will cover this in more detail in the chapter on Tenacity. We must make a concerted effort to surround ourselves with the proper "voices", who will help us push through with courage during difficult times.

One last note: There is genuine clinical depression. If you have depression, you should visit a doctor. Just as if you were to break your leg, you would visit a doctor for medical help, if you have depression, you need professional treatment.

Exercise 3. Choose your Courage Mirror that surrounds you.

Choose your environment that will be around you each day. Paintings, wall color, music, TV shows, travel, photos, furniture, books, poems and quotations and verses and "anchor phrases"[28] on the wall. What you speak to yourself today, is who you will likely be 5 years from now. My view of the most important step I can take in the next minute ... depends on my long-term view.

4 Hand of Virtue. Hold your 5 most important virtues.

Each year in February, Penn State holds a 46 hour dance marathon called THON.[29] Starting from small roots, THON has grown to be the largest student-run philanthropy in the world, in both personal involvement and in revenue. In 2013, THON raised over $12 million toward the cause of pediatric cancer, and since 1973, the event has raised over $100 million. Over 15,000 Penn State students were involved in 2013, including an enormous number of my own students in our Chemical Engineering Department. The motto is "FTK", or "For the Kids".

The funds from THON go to the Four Diamonds Fund, which is a charitable organization based out of Penn State's Hershey Medical Center. The Four Diamonds Fund was started in 1972 by Charles and Irma Millard, who lost their son Chris to pediatric cancer at the age of 14. Before his death, Chris wrote a fantasy story called *The Four Diamonds*, which eventually became a Disney TV movie. In the fantasy, knighthood conquers evil, and the teenage hero seeks to gather the "four diamonds" of Courage, Wisdom, Honesty and Strength. Chris Millard believed that these were the four virtues necessary for him to win his battle against cancer. Anyone who has attended the event, which is now held in the large Bryce Jordan Center, can attest to the power of every minute of the 46 hours.

Sometimes it is difficult to remember what we believe, when a critical moment arrives upon us. We "believe" in so many things, that we come to believe in practically nothing. We lose the strength required to respond forcefully to events in life. We fail to notice. My daughters sometimes walk with us through a nearby forest, where sometimes there are tiny, round, colored BBs on the ground, perhaps there from other children's play. When my girls saw their first BB, they became aware. Now each time we visit that forest, they find dozens of these BBs in a single walk.

What virtues will we take notice of? What are your most important virtues? There are dozens or even hundreds of potential virtues one could hold in esteem: faith, dignity, honesty, enthusiasm, courage, industry, loyalty, compassion, frugality, contentment, curiosity, risk-taking, patience, generosity, wisdom, strength, justice, righteousness[30], joy, peace[31]. What five virtues can you hold on the tips of your fingers, that you can call upon without hesitation and without blinking? Chris Millard knew his most important virtues. If you cannot choose one hand of 5 virtues, you can perhaps choose two hands' worth – but beware of diluting the power of one hand.

Having 25 virtues that are important to you, could mean that none is especially memorable or forceful in your life. Choosing just 5 virtues increase the power, so that you can respond to events in life with rapidity and resolve.

Exercise 4. Choose your top 5 virtues for the Hand of Virtue.

Choose the 5 virtues that you consider to be most important. What conditions in your life led to these 5 virtues being the most important to you? Just as diamonds are formed under conditions of high temperature and pressure, so your most important virtues will likely arise from such events, which might in fact be in your Scratch List. There are many books and documents written about virtues, which might help you clarify the most important ones for you.[32,33]

5 Eye of Dignity. See people as people, with dignity.

On the evening of April 4, 1968, my Dad was attending night school at the University of Cincinnati. During class, someone came into the room to tell the students, "Be careful out there tonight. Someone just shot Martin Luther King, Jr., and rioting is starting." That night, my Dad parked farther away from class than usual, in order to save money on parking. He wished he had not.

The next day, Jane Elliott, a 3rd-grade teacher in Riceville, Iowa, ran her famous "brown eyes / blue eyes" experiment.[34] The purpose of the experiment was to demonstrate to the students how racism starts and breeds. The essential idea – which still often forms the basis of diversity training – was that on Friday, Elliott told the class that recent research had shown that brown-eyed students are smarter. The brown-eyed students got extra privileges, and were treated better than the blue-eyed students. On Monday, Elliott reversed, telling the class that she had made a mistake in understanding the research, and that the blue-eyed students were smarter. Afterwards, she explained the exercise to the students. Many of the students, as well as Jane Elliott herself, came to see people differently. They came to realize that all people are in fact people, not objects to be put down.

How will you see people? The book *Leadership and Self-Deception*[35] discusses how one of the most significant self-deceptions we engage, is in treating ourself as "the person", and others as objects. Other people can fade from being actual persons, to objects, problems, nuisances, or threats. In some cases we come to ignore the plights of others. How powerful are the lines written by Martin Niemöller, which appear at the United States Holocaust Memorial Museum in Washington, D.C.:

> *First they came for the socialists,*
> > *and I didn't speak out because I wasn't a socialist.*
> *Then they came for the trade unionists,*
> > *and I didn't speak out because I wasn't a trade unionist.*
> *Then they came for the Jews,*
> > *and I didn't speak out because I wasn't a Jew.*
> *Then they came for me,*
> > *and there was no one left to speak for me.*

If we come to see others as important as ourselves, we recognize that an injustice to one is an injustice to all. And sometimes it happens that we are interacting with people who do not seem as they appear.[36] If we set up a "we versus them" perspective in our Character, we end up with "our half" and "the other half".[37]

Exercise 5. *Assess your Eye of Dignity.*

List people in your life with whom you interact often: spouse, children, family, friends, colleagues, and even enemies. Are they 1) energizing, generous, caring, 2) problems, nuisances, threats, or 3) stingy, inconsiderate, uncaring? You will likely think of more adjectives or labels. Now for each of the people you mentioned, write where they stand on a scale from being a "person" (10) to an "object" (0), in your heart. And also list one thing that you could do to help that would show that person you care deeply for them. Would you do it, if the opportunity arose, without reservation? If so, you are on your way to having an eye of dignity toward that person. If not, you might be "in the box",[38] trapped into self-interested thinking, and Reference 38 might be very helpful.

Action Checklist

☐ **Scratch List.** List of 3-10 deep scratches in your life. You might want to *choose* and engage a *new* scratch that you would *like* to have, to build your character "on purpose". This could involve travel, a retreat, a conference, or a volunteer position for instance, for self, family, marriage, venture, career, or other.

☐ **Life Ring.** Draw your Life Ring on one sheet of paper, using a template like that on the next page. First choose a picture that represents your "master in the middle". Then list all the arenas of your life – self, family, work, community, clubs, and anywhere else where you spend time. Take time to narrow these to 5 to 9 arenas, which might require important decisions. Finally, in each arena, list 2 to 5 *habits* that you will pursue each week, to support that arena.

☐ **Courage Mirror.** Choose 3-10 photos, paintings, poems, songs, or other pieces to place around you, in the space that you live. The purpose of the Courage Mirror is to speak to you the "right voices", which gives you courage as you journey through life toward the person you authentically want to become. The selection of these pieces is an experimental process, and the pieces might well change with time.

☐ **Hand of Virtue.** List the 5 most important virtues in your life. Include a story about why each is important.

☐   **Eye of Dignity.** List people in your life with whom you interact
    often, and consider whether you categorize them under a label.
    Is each of these people more of a person to you … or an object?

Creating a draft of the information in this checklist might require
just a few hours, and have significant benefits. If you find that to
make reasonable progress takes longer, that is OK too. Either way,
in working through the elements of this process, you will identify,
and start to change, your own Character. Give yourself permission
to be more authentically you, which might include giving yourself
permission to dream, to fail, to celebrate, to rest.

Life Ring Template

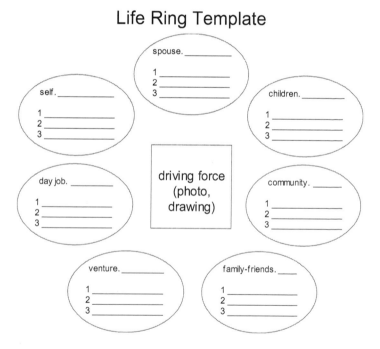

Here are some suggested additional readings:

- a sacred text. Bible, Quran, Vedas, Feynmann Lectures on Physics. Whatever is sacred for you.
- Arbinger Institute, *Leadership and Self-Deception: Getting out of the Box.* (2010). This book takes great strides in distinguishing being "in the box" – deceived by self-interest – and "out of the box".
- Assaraf, John; and Murray Smith. *The Answer: Grow Any Business, Achieve Financial Freedom, and Live an Extraordinary Life.* Atria Books (2009). Assaraf and Smith define a "vision board", which is type of classic visualization theory.
- *Autobiography of Martin Luther King, Jr.*
- Bennett, William J. *The Book of Virtues.* (1996). This book lists numerous virtues, and gives poems, fables, and stories to support them.
- Ferriss, Timothy, *The 4-Hour Workweek.* In his acronym "DEAL", the "D" is for "define". How will you define the life you want? His "D" is helped by having the appropriate Courage Mirror.
- Gandhi, Mohandas Karamchand (Mahatma), *Autobiography: The Story of My Experiments with Truth.*
- Walton, Mary. *A Woman's Crusade: Alice Paul and the Battle for the Ballot.* (2010).
- Hybels, Bill. *Holy Discontent: Fueling the Fire That Ignites Personal Vision.* (2007). Outstanding book for seeing how a "Scratch List" can lead to vision.

Entrepreneurship

The country needs and, unless I mistake its
temper, the country demands bold, persistent
experimentation. It is common sense to take a
method and try it: If it fails, admit it frankly
and try another. But above all, try something.
– President Franklin Delano Roosevelt[39]

Entrepreneurship. I run smart experiments and take
smart risks toward my dream of _____.

In many of our lives, there comes a moment when we decide we want to "do something great". We have a vision of greatness. The vision might be in your career, or your family, or your community, or your children's grade school. The vision might be great in the eyes of a hundred people, a million, a billion … or two, or even one – yourself! You become absolutely energized by the vision.

There are various reasons why we take on these visions. Some of us simply stumble onto something that we find we are exceptionally capable at, right from the start. For whatever reason – it might involve physical attributes, observational skills, various experiences – we catch on quickly.

For others, a vision takes hold in their lives after they have enough experience. In reading biographies and autobiographies of great men and women, I often find that this occurs between the ages of 35 and 45, and requires about 15 years of experience. These people reach an unsettling transition point – a "crossroads moment"

– where they desire to do something great. Sometimes this is a called a "midlife crisis".

For still others, necessity requires that they make a change. When "times are good", everybody can win, and all organizations can find enough resources. When times get tight – perhaps a new competitor arrives on the seen – then one must turn to new methods for survival. I wrote the following note to some friends in Summer 2013:

Dear Friends,

In the 1950s, my Grandpap Velegol was a big coal mine businessman, owning many mines, trucks, and equipment, and having many employees. The residential coal business was huge. It would last forever. And then oil and gas heating came along, and residential coal died.

In the 1970s my Dad was an engineer at Weirton Steel. 12,000 employees. Union jobs coming faster than anyone knew how to handle. It would last forever. Then came other materials, and other competitors. By the late 1990s, the company had essentially died. My Dad was retired, but had a lot of headaches with his pension and medical plans.

In the 2010s, Darrell is a professor at Penn State University. 44,000 students at University Park, large tuitions. Universities are about research and teaching, of critical importance. Students strive to get a coveted spot in our classrooms and earn our degrees. It will last forever ...

Have a great day! Darrell

While the University system tends to have a very stable structure, as I write this in 2013, I can see broad changes on the way. This Fall 2013 I am teaching a MOOC (massive open online course) in "Creativity, Innovation, and Change". We have more than 100,000 students enrolled, more than exist in the entire Penn State system right now. Yes, I see changes coming ...

Change is often driven by "change makers", or entrepreneurs. I think of Rowland Hill using penny postage to reform the British postal system,[40] Florence Nightingale using statistical methods to enhance the quality of nursing care, Craig Venter using his shotgun sequencing approach to map the human genome,[41] Luciano Pavarotti effortlessly singing nine high C's in *La Fille du Régiment*,[42] Muhammad Yunus developing systems for microfinance to become a "banker to the poor".[43]

The most significant enemy of entrepreneurship, and advancing forward, is *fear*. We fear rejection; we fear loss; we doubt our abilities. As Shakespeare wrote,[44]

> *Our doubts are traitors,*
> *And make us lose the good we oft might win*
> *By fearing to attempt.*

Will you dare to attempt? As the Chapter on Tenacity discusses, you will need to surround yourself with the right voices, and as the Chapter on Character discusses, you need to surround yourself with the right images.

Once we recognize how to manage our fear, how then do we manage – or drive – all this change? When do we find time to make the changes, since life doesn't stop at the moment when change is needed or desired? Entrepreneurship is the answer. It is about undertaking a new ventures. Indeed, the etymology of the word is the French *entrependre*, which means "to undertake".   An entrepreneur organizes, manages, and assumes the risks of a business or enterprise. My friend Brian Cunningham, himself a very successful entrepreneur, says that entrepreneurship is "The relentless pursuit of opportunity independent of resources presently controlled." In this chapter we will examine the tools that will help in the practice of Entrepreneurship. We will discover how to stake out your space, come up with ideas, and start.

1 Venture. Set time to expose yourself to the game.

In 1887, Milton Snavely Hershey started the Lancaster Caramel Company.[45] He used a caramel recipe he had learned from others, and his caramel company became a significant success story. However, Milton Hershey soon developed an even bigger game he wanted to enter: the milk chocolate business. In the early 1900s, milk chocolate was a luxury item, and Hershey sought to find a way to enter the business and become the leader.

In 1900 Hershey sold the Lancaster Caramel Company to the American Caramel Company for $1 million, and got into the milk chocolate business. Hershey established the company in what is now Hershey, Pennsylvania, amidst many large dairy farms, where he could purchase the milk required for his confection. He was a relentless experimentalist, himself trying many different recipes and techniques to develop a process for mass producing inexpensive, storable milk chocolate. One of the key developments he oversaw was the use of sweet condensed milk, which enabled him to store the chocolate for much longer periods. The first Hershey's Bar was mass produced in 1900, and within a few years, Hershey established one of the largest milk chocolate factories in the world. He had entered the game, run countless experiments, and in the end, "won the game." Hershey Chocolate is currently the largest chocolate producer in North America.

Hershey made time to try a new venture, and then explored it. Starting new ventures requires significant time – usually at least 20% or more of your normal "work time". Some companies, such as Google, encourage their employees to take one day per week to work on a new idea in the company. All the other skills under "Entrepreneurship" depend upon your making enough time to "play at your new game". And remember, the opposite of play is not work – the opposite of play is depression![46] With time, you might find a game at which you have some skill, and which energizes you! Working at these games will usually give peace, not anxiety.

At some point, if you find that you are good at one of "your games", seek to find or create an organization that competes at the event. You are looking to find a competition where you can practice and test your skills against others. As Agatha Christie, the famous author, once said, "The secret to getting ahead, is getting started." At the same time, you might need to prune or let go of the other games, until you re-adjust your schedule; we will discuss pruning, and the grieving process associated with it, in the chapter on "owNership".

How does a person find the time to play at these ventures, which are critical to making advances in life? Ambitious people typically have full schedules, don't they? Yes. Under the chapter on "owNership", we will discuss more strategies for setting aside 10-20% of your resources so that you have the ability to play, find a venture that you can excel at, and expand that game in your life. Keep in mind that shifting sands – whether in your family, your job, your community – often require that we spend a significant amount of time maintaining or putting out fires. If you're trying to innovate on top of this, that requires a lot of extra effort! For brief periods, you might be able to adjust and do "two jobs". Keep in mind that this is a short-term strategy which is sometimes necessary. When it happens, you need to start looking for how you can eliminate one of the day jobs.

Another important point is that you "give yourself permission" to play at what I love to do.[47] Many of us learned in school that we had to ask for permission for everything – even going to the bathroom – and that we were not allowed to try and not succeed, else we would get a "C" grade, or maybe even an "F". We also became addicted to being taught, always expecting that an all-knowing teacher had all the answers. But now I ask, will you give yourself permission to advance in life, and to try for an "A", even if you know you might fail badly? Will you believe that you can learn by yourself, if no teacher is there? These are critical traits.

As you play at your venture, keep practicing and stretching, within your "zone of proximal development".[48] Stretch, but not too far. Play hard, without wearing yourself out. We will tackle how to deal with being overwhelmed, and how to evaluate ideas, later.

How does one evaluate whether to continue at a venture or game? First, does the effort energize you, or drain you, most of the time. If you look ahead, and find that if you had full success in the venture, but you feel absolutely *drained* ... then oftentimes, the best thing to do is to get out of that game.[49] As often as possible with entrepreneurial activities, find ventures that energize you. Second, oftentimes it is helpful to find ventures that match some aspect of your ability set. You need some competitive advantage to win a game. Third, make sure the venture matches your values; otherwise, you set yourself up for hard choices down the road.

Earlier in this chapter, I mentioned that I very often see people reach their crossroads moment between the ages of 35 and 45, although not always. When that happens, engage in organized competition, so that you can play and practice playing against others to see if you truly have enough skill to play eventually at a high level. It is very important that at some point, you *start*. Before you can receive your purpose, you often must try various ventures. You might soon find that your "play job" ... can also become your "day job".

Exercise 6. Embark on 1-2 Ventures, and play those games.

List and describe briefly one or two new ventures that you will try. Enjoy playing at these games, and give yourself permission to play, even if you play badly at first. It is OK. If possible, identify a way to compete or participate in the game or Venture. Your game could be learning to write poetry, starting a business, joining a book club, playing pickup softball, running for elected office – anything. You might start a game that addresses the deep needs of people, that allows you to address their *pain*. Sometimes it is useful to work at several games at once. I often find that I am playing at a game for a while before I even realize it, but at some point, I usually declare that I am playing a game – and right now, I am thinking about my work with Wild Scholars[50] education, and the book I wrote about this new way of thinking about education – and I choose a start date.

2 Fences. Establish boundaries, with gates.

A study has been reported that sought to find how pre-school kids play at a playground, either with a fence or without.[51] One playground had no fence, while the other similar playground had a fence. At recess, the kids went to one playground one day, and the other playground another day. On the playground with the fence, the kids played right up to the boundary. How far beyond that region would the kids play, when the fence was not there? Surprisingly ... the kids ended up huddling closer to the center! That is, when the fence was not there, the kids explored *less* of the playground!

This story suggests an important principle: the "paradox of structure". Can a fence, paradoxically, make us more likely to explore a *larger* region? And if so, can we ever get "beyond the fence"? Is structure necessary to creativity[52] and developing new ideas? These structures include time management, budgeting, templates for producing documents or landscapes or products, methods for distributing work, and others. These structures are related to some ideas in the "ownership" chapter, but I list them here, because without them, the ability to create new ideas is actually impeded! It is a paradox of structure in creativity: We might think at first that having no structure maximizes creative ability, but in fact the opposite is true! Some structure is needed.

There are two key limitations to innovation, in the absence of clear structures for time-energy-money-processes-reputation. 1) Fear. Without a fence, we might be afraid to explore beyond a certain region. These fences provides boundaries for how much money we can spend, how much time we can give, how much energy we will devote, how much reputation we will put on the line. Without a knowledge of the boundaries, we are often afraid to commit resources. 2) Dispersion. Without a fence, our minds can wander in too many directions, and our time-energy-money are dispersed, never producing a coherent result. We engage distractions, rather than high value problems.

Say that you are planning your daughter's birthday party. If you establish at the outset that you need to keep the party to less than $100, that it will last 2 hours, and that we will have two friends, those three boundaries will enable you to plan the games, cake, presents, and other parts of the party much more readily, than if you simply decide to "plan a party". Furthermore, if you set these limits and your daughter understands them, she will help you to plan to the party in a much more helpful manner.

At the same time, we must balance structure with open-ness. We need to establish "gates" within the fence, because otherwise you might miss important opportunities. For example, to the birthday planning, you might add, "If we can make the party include six friends for just $25 more, we will explore that." We have included a gate in the boundary.

Exercise 7. Establish clear Fences, with gates.

Set boundaries for the resources in your life, for a given Life Ring arena, habit, project, or other category. What is the range of money you will spend? What is the minimum and maximum amount of time you will spend? At what point will you allow your reputation to be invested, and when will it be enough? If you are entering a new arena – with self, family, work, community – what rules exist that provide natural boundaries? Perhaps there are legal rules, or perhaps there are unwritten rules. You need to find that fence, so that you know the "safe" regions to traverse. At the same time, it is useful to have gates that you can open at appropriate times to enter new territory. It is a "paradox of structure": Having some structure actually *increases* the amount of entrepreneurial work.

3 Idea Journal. Observe and reflect by habit.

In the mid-1990s, I was a PhD student at Carnegie Mellon University in Pittsburgh. Early on, I was looking for an idea upon which to build my PhD, something that would take roughly three or four years of dedicated work. One night I went to bed, tired from trying experiments in the lab. Normally I am a very sound sleeper, but at some point in the middle of the night, I awoke from my sleep and had an idea for my thesis. The idea was use electrophoresis, a phenomenon our lab studied, to measure forces between colloidal particles. At that point in my life, I was not accustomed to waking with a "grand idea", but for whatever strange reason, I was lucid enough to get out of bed and write down the idea. That night, I awoke several more times, with additional ideas, and each time I got out of bed and wrote down the idea on a sheet of paper.

When I awoke in the morning, I had a plan for an outstanding PhD right in front of me! As a PhD student, I had learned how to keep a good lab notebook, which contains all of the observations, data, experimental details, analysis, and reflections from work in the lab. But this new concept -- of writing down ideas as they come -- was a somewhat new concept to me. It was the first time I can recall using what I now know -- from Jack Matson's work -- as an "idea journal". Over the next few years, I worked the plan -- including past many hurdles -- and made it happen. But all this work was based on the plan from that first night. In 1998 my PhD thesis won the Victor K. LaMer Award for outstanding PhD in Colloid and Surface Science from the American Chemical Society. My thesis and this award played a big part in my getting my position on the faculty of Penn State in Chemical Engineering.

So what is an idea journal? What are its benefits, and what are the challenges in keeping one? Idea journals resolve two significant problems.

1 forgetting. We often forget events that we do not record. The act of recording helps with memory, and the written word is there when we review the idea journal. We forget not only the facts or ideas, but we also forget the history and feeling we had. And not only do we remember the idea, but we tend to organize it better, as we keep an idea journal for longer.

2 habits of observation-reflection-creativity. If we do not have habits in the areas of observation-reflection-creativity, our abilities in these areas suffer. We need practice for those areas of our lives that will thrive, and observation-reflection-creativity are no exceptions. We build the habit of reflection and analysis.

The solution is to develop the *habit* of keeping an idea journal. There are two key benefits:

1 recording ideas. By recording ideas, we remember the facts and concepts. We can also review historically our path for an idea, so that we do not mis-remember our feelings and passion about particular events. If an idea comes up 10 times over 3 years, it might be something that "scratches" us, that we have an underlying passion to change. Events of the day or smooth voices can make us forget the scratches, unless we have written them down.

2 practice . The very habit of keeping an idea journal improves our skills of observation and reflection. It inspires new ideas, and helps us to recognize connections. My ears are always open to new ideas, and I often make a brief numerical analysis of a problem with my notebook.   I keep track of ideas, websites, contacts (email and phone).

Exercise 8. Start and grow an Idea Journal.

There are three primary action steps for this exercise on "Idea Journal".

1 idea journal. Keep an idea journal. How to keep it? Usually ... in a simple way, that you will use each day and carry with you always. In my own case, I carry an audio voice recorder[53] with me at all times. This is a small device (e.g., an Olympus VN-702PC or Sony ICD-PX820, or one of the newer variants to these, which typically cost $50) that has 5 voice folders, labelled A-E. Here is how I use mine:

A for urgent notes, daily "to do", big ideas.

B for spiritual notes

C for notes on any book I am listening to at the moment

D for notes on any book (2nd folder)

E for notes on education or entrepreneurship

The "A" folder might include items like "sign up for ACS conference" to "get eggs" to "plan anniversary dinner". I keep folders C and D because I listen to many books from www.audible.com, and I keep notes in the recorder. At the end of the day, I transcribe these notes into my computer, keeping the date and circumstances, and my own feelings. Where do I find the time? Typically I have 10-20 notes in a day, and I can usually type these into my computer in 5 minutes.

Jack Matson keeps actual "journals" -- bound books in which he writes his notes throughout the day. A number of friends I know use this simple but powerful method. And many of us keep "idea cards", which might be 3x5 cards or business cards that we keep in our pocket with a pen, to write down ideas as they come along. In my case I type in these ideas at the end of the day, along with my audio recorder. I keep the cards because there are some locations where you cannot use the audio recorder as easily, such as in some meetings.

2 habit. Build the habit of recording in an idea journal. For example, especially as you begin the practice, you might measure yourself on the number of ideas you write each day, maybe 5 or 10 new ideas, and the number of actions you take. Curiosity, and the habit of asking questions, is a habit that can be built.

3 distill. Periodically, I review my notes, and pull out the best ones into a selected location. Over time, there are certain ideas that get repeated, and some that just keep rising to the top of the list. These ideas are "evaluating well" over time. The review step also helps to keep my memory of past events sharp, so that when new ideas come along, I am prepared to receive them. This connection step happens quite frequently.

4 Failure Resume. List your glorious failures

My students at Penn State all have resumes that they write, in order to secure job offers. They list their high GPAs if they have them, their successful projects, their extracurricular activities, their internships and coop experiences. They do not list a resume like this one, which is for an actual person:

- No high school or college degree.
- Started a store, which landed in debt.
- Ran for political office several times, unsuccessfully.
- Proposed for marriage, and turned down.

There are a number of other events in the life of this "loser" – whom we now know as the 16th President of the United States, Abraham Lincoln. One reason why so few of us are qualified to be leaders, is that our "failure resume" is not daring enough.

What will be your failure resume? Will you try for events with a big enough challenge, that there is a likelihood that you will fail? Will you place yourself in uncomfortable or even dangerous situations, so that you can grow? George Washington wrote that the Marquis de Lafayette was "determined to be in the way of danger". Will you be in the way of danger, with your time, energy, money, honor, fortune, or even life? Once in March 2012 when I visited Hollywood Studios with my family, I heard Walt Disney say on a recording, "I think it's important to have a good hard failure when you're young."

My good friend and mentor Jack Matson recommends that we all develop a failure resume, both to keep us humble, and to celebrate the fact that failure is necessary to success. On my own failure resume, I might include that I tried out for the high school baseball team, and was cut. I wrote a letter to train with a prominent piano teacher at West Virginia University, and never even received a reply letter. I tried for a Rhodes Scholarship, got to the Region 2 finals … and lost. I was engaged to be married, and it did not happen. I have applied for dozens of grants at Penn State, and only about 1 in 10 get funded. In short, I have failed failed failed. But I have tried. And as a result, my stack of successes is satisfying to me.

Exercise 9. List your biggest failures on a Failure Resume.

Write a resume that includes your most spectacular failures! Where do you want successes – which might end up as evidence that you tried and failed? List any relevant details, as you would in listing the usual "successes" of a resume. Aim at challenges that you can "win", not at events where you "won't lose". That is, focus on challenges, not threats, and you will find the courage to risk rejection. As Sir Ken Robinson says, "You must become comfortable with the possibility of failure."[54]

5 One Percent Experiments. Plant seeds and "IFF".

Dick Fosbury revolutionized the high jump.[55] Early in his high school tenure as a high jumper, Fosbury sometimes could not make the qualifying height to compete. About 5 years later, as he competed in the 1968 Olympics in Mexico City, Fosbury won the gold medal and set a new record of 2.24 meters. What was the difference? It was the "Fosbury flop", the back-first technique of jumping over the higher bar. Fosbury invented the technique, and then ran experiment after experiment, including the run up to the bar, that enabled him to make this revolution into a viable technique.

How do we run smart experiments and take smart risks? One key is to properly understand "risk". Around 2010, our department invited one of our alumni, William H. Joyce, to speak with our faculty in Chemical Engineering. He had served as President and CEO of Union Carbide, and later, Hercules Corporation. Joyce's message was based on "understanding risk". He started, "Most people do not have a proper understanding of risk. They think that if I invest $1000, and get a $100 return on average, that if I invest $100, I should get a $10 return on average, and if I invest $1 million, I should get a $100,000 return on average." But he pointed out that risk doesn't work that way! Our normal mindset is "proportional", so that the rate of return is fixed regardless of the risk of investment.

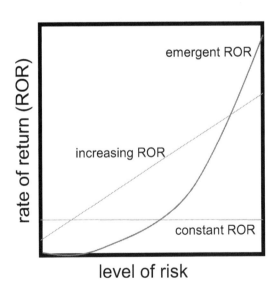

He pointed out that rate of return (ROR) actually increases with risk. That is, if I risk $1, my return might be 2 cents, not 10 cents. And if I invest $10 million, I might expect a $1.4 million return, more than the $1 million of a constant ROR mindset. As CEO, he chose to risk as high as he could, without taking the company under if the investment went sour. He was encouraging us as faculty to take risks as large as we could, in order to maximize return. As achievers, faculty often take low risks, and receive a low ROR. On the other hand, entrepreneurs take higher risks, and on average earn a higher ROR. And both are distinguished from gamblers, who have a "lottery mentality"[56] and take risks with a negative payback on average, even though at times they might win.

Of course, we need to take smart risks. Jack Matson, an expert in creativity, wrote an outstanding book called *Innovate or Die*. In the book, he discusses a principle that he developed, called "Intelligent Fast Failure" (IFF). In the book, he describes how we are so reluctant to embrace failure as a learning tool, and so we get stuck, unable to move forward. As Tony Dungy, the Super Bowl winning football coach, has said, "Remember that failure isn't part of your identity; it's part of your journey."[57] At the same time, you want to fail early, small, rapidly, and cheap, rather than late, big, slow, and expensive. The "fast" part of IFF is that once we know a large fraction of what we are able to know without trying, it is time to "run the experiment". Do it right away – there is no benefit to waiting! Run a rapid prototype. At the same time, we need to learn from those failures, and that is the "intelligent" part. IFF became a way of life for Jack, and for many of us disciples who learned from him. We set out "to IFF".

In running experiments, we must recognize two types of failure or mistakes. The first mistake is a mistake of ambition. Here we must know the tolerance for failure. There is a different tolerance level for a NASA space flight,[58] and a family breakfast time, and a new product rollout. But the principle still holds that we must fail early, small, rapidly, and cheap. What changes is what we mean by early, small, rapidly, and cheap. The second type of mistake is a mistake of sloth[59], when we refuse to change because we are afraid, even when we know the facts. As I once heard Bill Joyce say, "It is not about *taking* risks. It is about *identifying* risks, and *managing* the risks." "Taking risks" has the feel of proceeding without thinking, whereas managing risk assesses the known, acknowledges the unknown, and proceeds to within tolerances.

In *The Lean Startup*,[60] the author discusses the importance of trying experiments and learning rapidly. He promotes the "build-measure-learn" style of learning.[61] Create products or services that can be used by those who need them (build), let those whom you want to serve try them while you take measurements (measure), and then then return to the drawing board to assess the lessons and change the product or service (learn). Don't simply guess; set up actual experiences for those whom you want to serve, and as much as possible, take *quantitative* measurements[62]. Create "rapid prototype" products that you can get to clients quickly, so that you can gain feedback quickly. Sometimes these products are called MPVs, or "minimal viable products", to indicate that you want to get the minimal essence into the product or service, so that you can test it rapidly. At my daughters' school, they call these the "sloppy copy". You are not aiming to be sloppy, but early on, it is the best you can do. Learning is the key goal for 1% experiments, and as Lou Holtz, the famous college football coach, likes to say, "Luck follows speed." Learn quickly!

One important aspect of experiments is that they allow you to evaluate your ideas, which you explore week-by-week in your venture. You will move naturally toward successes, and you might well find that successful areas of your ventures start to crowd out your "day job", whether that is with family, work, or community.

Usually that is OK, and even preferable! Go where your energy is leading you. Of course, you need to check this movement with your Hand of Virtue and your Life Ring, but in general, you will do your best when you follow your energy, thinning out to keep the very best ideas. A process for thinning ideas and tasks is nicely-provided in the book *The Pumpkin Plan*, by Mike Michalowicz.[63]

As you learn, you will systemize your findings, as discussed under the "Systems" tool under owNership. On balance, you will explore with Enrepreneurship, gain new skills with Excellence, and when you have successes, systemize them with owNership. This helps you to lock in the gains you have made, giving Jim Collins' flywheel effect. For many readers, you might start by spending 15-20% of your time in each of the CENTER practices, in order to both grow and solidify that growth. If you run too many experiments, you might not have enough resources to carry on with your "day job", which provides necessary resources. If you run too few experiments, you will lack the needed learning and growth to keep up with a changing world.

Exercise 10. Identify and run small 1% experiments.

Aim toward your minimal viable product (MVP) – which is a type of grand experiment – and in so doing, write a list of the top five 1% experiments that you will run, in order to learn rapidly. The key to a great experiment, is a clearly-defined problem. The experiment must be set up so that at its end, you will know the answer to your problem or question. Not only does a clear problem enable you to learn the information you need, but also whether your experiment tells you want you want or not, the learning process is a success! That enables you to make your identity as an "experimenter", mapping the unknown.

In running experiments in life, you must be willing to fail or be wrong[64]. And while sometimes you will have a team, often you must step out alone. This is part of the essence of IFF. At the same time, you can avoid the label of "failure", which we sometimes attach to ourselves if we don't see the true outcome of the experiment as learning. In the end you will have not just a tolerance of failure, but a hungry appetite for it, knowing its value in mapping the unknown.

I emphasize the important of aiming at your MVP, which is an entire design or scenario. In Jack Matson's "intelligent fast failure", the idea is not simply to fail at every step by brute force, but to intelligently design the entire scenario or product or service, and then as one learns, to update the scenario. That keeps your mind focused on the entire system.

6 Spare Diamonds. Use slack resources creatively.

"Acres of Diamonds" is a famous speech written by Russell Conwell in 1890. He delivered the speech over 5000 times, and he made enough money from it to start Temple University. The essence of the speech is that there is wealth right in our own "back yard", and we just have to find it. This speech has inspired millions of people to make fortunes. Conwell thought of it as a duty for each of us to maximize our wealth, in order that we can help the common good.

Most of us have not found any diamond mines on our property, nor even any bags of money or gold. So where are these acres of diamonds? Let me distinguish between a "lottery mentality" – where you find great riches with no effort – and what I see in the "acres of diamonds" speech.[65] A lottery mentality is self-focused, thinking only of leisure and ease. The "acres of diamonds" mentality is one focused on finding what others need, and filling that need. What if there is no money in the work? All the better! As Derek Sivers says,[66] it is an advantage to have a venture in which no money is available at first ... it likely means you have fewer competitors!

Where do we find these diamonds? If we want to advance in our ventures, we must have slack resources. And to find them, we must look in the right places. In the Summer of 2012, my daughter and I were looking for sand clams at the beach in Ocean City, New Jersey. When we were at the beach about 20 feet above the water line, we found none. But as we approached the places where the waves were crashing in, we found many! We didn't even have to dig! Oftentimes, when you are striving in places where the waters are a bit rougher, you will find resources more readily.

Where are those places in your life? Is there a labor market around you, people who want to do great things with their life, and are looking for mentorship? This is my situation at Penn State University, where hungry students are eager to help with important work, for course credits. It is a win-win situation, since they have the unique opportunity to work with faculty on important projects, while we have the opportunity to work with energetic, bright students for free, or for low wages. Do you have unique natural resources, such as land or water? Do you have a high density of population in your area? Do you have excess radio time capacity? Do you have extra skilled persons? Do you have a special kinship among the people in your organization? Usually, it is difficult to find "extra money" lying around. But it is often easier to find other types of resources that others do not recognize as being valuable ... yet.

In Spring and Summer of 2013, we were preparing to have our first MOOC, massive-open-online-course, in "Creativity, Innovation, and Change". Over 100,000 students enrolled. How do we support that effort? Our initial approach was to write a budget for $500,000, and work to fund it. The leadership above us was very uncomfortable with that! And so we had to be creative. We started finding interns for technical help, students at Penn State to help with taking video, graduate students for teaching assistants who wanted to be part of a MOOC so they could learn how to do it. In the end there were some real expenses for the course, but we were able to reduce the budget to less than 25% of the original amount.

Earlier we discussed another important spare diamond: time. You must take care to set aside time in order to conduct your venture. If you are too tight on any given resource – time, energy, money – and have no slack, you might improve your efficiency a bit, but you will lose many important opportunities. For the MOOC I just wrote about, we were passionate about it, and squeezed out other parts of our work in order to spend more time on our venture. Systemized work – I call this our "day job" – is often used to feed resources to our venture. But I find that to do revolutionary work, which can achieve growth of 2 times or even 10 times, one needs to set aside the benefits of systematic work such as higher pay and more respect in the short term, in order to allow the incubation time necessary for transformative work.

Exercise 11. Identify un-noticed Spare Diamonds resources.

Make a list of the following potential diamonds, and seek whether any of them applies to your situation:

- friends. Do any have skills that could help you?
- interns. Is there "excess skill" looking for experience?
- space. Do you have excess space at home, or in the office?
- land. Is there park land or side-walk space you can use?
- tools. Have extra power tools or machinery or electronics?
- internet. Is there an open web site you can access?
- knowledge. Do you have useful, but un-used, knowledge?
- frequent flyer miles. Got extra? Friends with extra?

How can you employ these and other "spare diamonds" to a venture? Remember, it is often more difficult to find "spare money" lying around. However, these other diamonds often lie un-unused, until someone sees a need for them. Find value, where others do not.

7 Serendipity. Master the luck by getting off the wheel.

Jack Matson has spent much of his adult life developing small businesses that are driven by creative ideas. When I asked Jack about how he "mastered the luck", and what are the key challenges, he responded, "Many people are caught up in their immediate busyness. They are always on the rapidly-turning wheel of life, spinning around. But it is important to get off the wheel, so that you can watch it as an external observer, so that you can anticipate where the wheel will be. Anticipating great moments, wherever you are, is one way to master the luck."

"Darrell, you no doubt remember being on the Engineering Faculty Council at Penn State with me. That committee had 30 people and was usually fairly dull. But each time I came, I was anticipating that something great would happen. At the one meeting when I raised an idea for a proposal that was being offered, when everyone else was ready to proceed without the idea, you alone stood with me in championing the idea. In that case, the idea was good, but our collaborative work has been even bigger. If I hadn't anticipated that something great might happen, even at something as normally-dull as that EFC meeting, it might not have happened."

"Mastering the luck" is serendipity. It is being open to possible surprises, so that when the opportunity arises, you are ready. Serendipity happens not as much when you are expecting a particular result – which can in fact *close* your mind – but simply when you are expecting that something great might happen. Awareness is the essential ingredient.

Tool 12. Anticipate moments of Serendipity.

Mastering the luck is about anticipating great moments. There is a fine line between anticipating great moments, perhaps even in particular areas, and expecting particular results, which can actually close your mind to new opportunities.

To improve your "luck" in the coming week, think about events you have coming – even dull events – and visualize the people who will be there. List these on a sheet of paper. Imagine seeing them, and having them raise an opportunity, or seeing them bring a resource, or having them introduce you to someone new and important or interesting. This visualization will help you to master the luck, as you raise your awareness.

8 Leadership Window. Move when the window opens.

In my senior year at West Virginia University, we had a class project in which all of us worked on a single design project. We elected one Chief Engineer. At that point, I had had few leadership roles.   But for that project, I was ready!   I love Chemical Engineering, solving equations, creating designs, working with other dedicated people. Those qualities did not enable me to become captain of my baseball team, class president, or head drummer of the marching band. But for our senior project, I found myself in the right place at the right time.[67] I was elected Chief Engineer. Did I contribute at all? Yes, I let others know I felt I was right for the position, and set up some of my own "small winds"[68], and planted seeds with other students and faculty.   But more than that, preparation met opportunity, and suddenly, I was the leader. At the time, I knew little about leading a group of 20 plus colleagues, but I read a number of books[69] and was able to make the transition successfully.

That is often how leadership arises. A person has life experiences and life skills – and often is not even aiming to have a leadership position – and suddenly finds herself or himself in a position to take charge. As Victor Hugo once said, "There is one thing stronger than all the armies in the world, and that is an idea whose time has come." If you pursue what you love to do, such that you have a measure of success at it, you don't need to seek leadership; it will seek you! Here is a useful equation:

venture = story + system

Build your story now. Get involved with what drives you most, as given in your Life Ring. Gestate that story. Nurture that story. And then at some point, a crisis will likely arise, for which you are exactly the right person to lead. Crisis gives birth to many ventures, whether in the family, in business, in sports, or in politics. As Kingdon points out for the political arena, progress happens when the problem, the solution, and the political will all intersect.[70] This happens somewhat rarely, but when it does, it is magical. The window of opportunity will open for a time … and then close – perhaps forever. Leaders must be ready.

When the crisis emerges, including in many cases fear and urgency, keep that fire alive, bring in your story and experience, and catch the existing wave. It is hard to "create the wave" – the opportunity[71] – but when you look out, feel the breezes, and see it coming, start swimming so that you are mobilized when the wave arrives. Once you are moving your story with the crisis, then finish the second part of the equation above: build systems. These systems include people, finances, workflow, whatever you need, so that the known parts of the work start to proceed automatically. Systems are the way that progress is captured and carried forward, and they are discussed much more in the Chapter on owNership. They enable the "flywheel effect" that Jim Collins wrote about in *Good to Great*.

Once you are called forward, you must choose whether you will do it. Some would consider it a responsibility to step forward and lead, even if you do not want to. That is your decision. The more common mistake is to avoid "giving away" your leadership product or service. We have a tendency to not want to "just let others have our art". More often than not, the opposite approach is valuable: Hasten to give it away! If people around you love what you are providing, very soon the demand will exceed the supply, and a market will arise … and you will be the supplier.

One last point about the Leadership Window comes from President Abraham Lincoln.

The dogmas of the quiet past, are inadequate to the stormy present. The occasion is piled high with difficulty, and we must rise – with the occasion. As our case is new, so we must think anew, and act anew. – Annual Message to Congress, 1862.

Sometimes we must change the rules of the game, in order to advance! Sometimes we must defy our teachers or leaders, to advance. And there is an important distinction between being a bit irreverent, and being rude. Are you willing to reach the defiant moment with the person who got you where you are?[72] Maybe a leader, a teacher, a parent? Will you defy them, to make the changes you know are best for people? That requires courage. And that is leadership. It is almost art itself. My PhD advisor, John L. Anderson, once told me, "Leadership is vision within constraints." But in his own career, he has often expanded the prevailing constraints, changing the rules through his effort. It is the essence of creative destruction.[73]

Here is a short list of people who changed the rules, often by reaching a defiant moment: George Washington and Thomas Jefferson (and others) with the American Revolution,[74] Montessori with "bad lads" in Italy, Ray Kroc with McDonalds, Milton Hershey with chocolate, Theodor Seuss Geisel with Dr. Seuss, Herb Simon with decision-making science, Martin Luther King Jr. with civil rights, Gandhi with human rights. Today's pioneers often become tomorrow's leaders, because they are mobilized when the wave arrives. You cannot always play by the old rules, since the people already in control made them! Revolutions can happen when tenacious work – often over many years or even decades – hits a tipping point with a crisis, and a courageous leader makes new rules.[75] When that opportunity comes, be ready to step forward, and when the defiant moment comes, change the rules of the game to help benefit many. Be ready.

Tool 13. Prepare for Leadership Window.

List 3-5 potential leadership windows. Only you will see this list, and so give yourself permission to be bold, rather than humble. As you live, and work on things you love to do, you are building a story. Gestating that story might take 5 years, or 10 years, or 15 years, or longer. The longer the gestation, often the bigger the birth. When that story meets a crisis, you might be set to become the leader. You can help a bit by creating your own interruptions and small winds, but mostly, the opportunity arrives.

Action Checklist

☐ **Venture.** Choose 1 or 2 new ventures that you will try in the coming year or quarter. Establish clear times during the week when you will "play" at your new venture, exposing yourself to a game so that you can learn rapidly.

☐ **Fences.** List the level of resources – especially time, energy, and money – that you are willing to invest in your new venture. List structures for how you will process work, software you will use, equipment management, and other aspects. As you figure out new ways of working, update your Structure to enable easier processing.

☐ **Idea journal.** Choose a method to record ideas throughout the day – perhaps an audio recorder, a small notebook, or a piece of paper. Keep track of ideas, observations, and contacts. Review them each semester.

☐ **Failure resume.** Make a resume of your greatest failures, using a format and style for which you might usually present your greatest triumphs. Then assess whether the failures are significant enough.

☐ **1% experiments.** Establish 5 experiments you can run, to enhance your learning about whether a particular idea will work or not. The experiments should be early in the venture, small enough not to sink the venture, fast, and cheap.

☐ **Spare diamonds.** List 5 or more resources available to you, that others might not see. Awareness that these resources exist, is what will enable you to find them. Look especially for non-monetary resources.

☐ **Mastering the luck.** For the next 3 days, before scheduled events happen, visualize first that something great might happen and what your feeling about that would be, and then anticipate particular areas where serendipity might arise.

☐ **Leadership window.** This tool is useful when a crisis hits, for which you are ready. Summarize 2 pages on how your story aligns with the crisis, and how can you systemize your effort to give a repeatable result. Also identify places where you will need to reach a defiant moment with others, and change the rules of the game.

Here are some suggested additional readings:

- Ferriss, Timothy, *The 4-Hour Workweek.* (2009).
- Matson, Jack V. *Innovate or Die: A Personal Perspective on the Art of Innovation.* (1996).
- Ries, Eric. *The Lean Startup: How Today's Entrepreneurs Use Continuous Innovation to Create Radically Successful Businesses.* (2011).

owNership

owNership. I choose _____, and then permit my agency to hustle, execute, and systemize.

My brother Dave Velegol – we usually call him "Duke" in our family – entered West Virginia University in 1984 to pursue a degree in Chemical Engineering. And he struggled his way through. "I must have been ranked #47 out of 48 students in our class," he says now with a laugh. When he looked for a job, he had great difficulty for 9 months. And then one day, he got an interview with a company near Pittsburgh. When Duke arrived at the interview, the interviewer threw down a 2 inch stack of resumes. "Dave, these resumes are for the senior position we are hiring for. Here is the stack for the entry level position." It was a single resume, my brother's. And so Duke got the job.

But there was a lot that Duke's GPA didn't say about him. Duke makes powerful choices toward great goals. He entered the design department at his company, and was willing to travel and delighted to interact with workers in the factories, whom he thought knew the real ins-and-outs of the operation. Soon he started bringing in new business. He made a choice to pursue a business degree, which his company paid for. Before long, he was doing jobs all over the world, and the company wanted someone who could roughly check contracts on the spot, without having to check every little piece with the company lawyers. Duke decided to enter law school, which the company paid for. These days, "Vice President Velegol" is making many of the major decisions in his company, growing it and expanding business. His rapid rise in the company happened because he made choices that others would not make, and then he worked very hard to make them happen. It also required the help of his family, including grandparents, who helped contribute to the effort. Duke did not allow his struggles in college trap him, but he made choices, and then executed on them.

Have you ever felt trapped by your circumstances? Do you feel like you are not able to do or think or speak as you choose? Perhaps you are living under a tyrant. Here are some tyrants that you might recognize in your own life:

- time. Is every minute of your time scheduled?
- energy. Do you always feel worn out?
- money. Are you buried in debt?
- what-if. Do you keep every bit of information, just in case?
- reputation. Do you feel trapped by expectations?
- precision. Does your precision thwart communication?
- capacity. Do you grab info or stuff, "just in case"?
- flood. Are you struggling beneath a flood of books, journals, emails, phone calls, appointments?
- people. Do you feel under the control of your boss ... or family or friends?

owNership in this book is *not* simply about owning stuff,[76] but rather, owNership is about taking charge of your own choices. In addition to the tyrants listed above, there is the tyranny of precedent, the tyranny of now, the tyranny of a mortgage, the tyranny of conscious thought, the tyranny of security, the tyranny of regulations. And of course, there is tyranny due to dictators and tyrants around the world. Nobody likes to be told what to do, or what to think. Do not give these tyrants authority to rule your life!

Victor Frankl, in his eye-opening book *Man's Search for Meaning*, discussed his imprisonment in a Nazi concentration camp. He came to realize at some point that between stimulus and response there is a space, where he could choose. By the end of World War II, Frankl saw himself as more free than the guards. As Stephen Covey said of this book, "Until I can say I am who I ame, because of the choices I made yesterday, I cannot say otherwise." There are at least three models for choosing: 1) Chaos says, "Nobody is in control. The decisions just happen." I call choices made randomly in this way "entropic choices". They have limited long-term effectiveness. 2) Determinism says, "Others are in control, and they choose." 3) Freedom says, "I am in control. I choose." Choosing and owNership from the perspective of freedom is a stance of proactivity.

Each of us has a supreme driving force. For some, it is family. For some, God. For some, the government. For some, fame. For some, science or rational thought. For some, justice. What or who is your master? That master forms the center of your Life Ring, and it comes deeply from your Character. Frankl discovered that it was his *choice*, who or what that master is in his own life. If you do not know your master, it will be difficult to make clear choices. And if you have 50 masters, your choices will often leave you feeling conflicted and confused.

Once you know your master, your choices spring from it. You might think, "That is easy to say, but if I don't please my boss, I'll lose my job and lose my home!" That might be true. Let us just declare then, that perhaps the security of your home or your family's comfort is your master? You might think, "That is all nice and good, but if I don't go with the crowd, I might be rejected as a friend." That might be true. Let us just declare then, that perhaps your friends or family or community is your master? And none of these choices is "wrong" – the choice is *yours*!

For this chapter, I will assume that you have made the difficult choices so that you know who or what is your master – your driving force in life – or that you are working on it. That is, I will assume for here that you have made progress in understanding your Character. It might be that most people never make the decision about who is their master. For those who do make the decision, it often takes years to come to grips with it, and realize it in their own life.

Knowing your Character, you are in a better position to make your choices. Of course, sometimes choosing is difficult. We need information and time to process, so that we can decide what are appropriate choices to satisfy or satisfice[77] our Character. But there is another important aspect of making choices: We often need to separate making the choice, from executing and systemizing the choice. Sometimes we know *what* we want, but we are afraid to proceed because we don't know *how* to go about making the choice.

One effective approach to executing and systemizing our choices is to "externalize your agency". Professor Lucky Yapa from Penn State's Geography Department talks about agency as "one's ability to do". In his work with the Philadelphia Field Project, he shows students that they have the ability to make great accomplishments – they have "agency". Later in this chapter we will see that by separating your choices from the execution of those choices – that is, externalizing your agency, you can greatly increase your effectiveness. A potential barrier is that sometimes we do not really give our agents permission to act on our behalf, even when we know the choice we have made! Give your agents the permission to act swiftly, once you have made your choice.

In large part having agency is the proactivity that Stephen Covey talked about in *7 Habits*, and Yapa moves this to a city-laboratory, where students can put the concepts into practice. owNership is your ability to make choices and champion your great ideas. Later you will have the chapter about Relationship, in which we will examine skills in working with others interdependently.

It is important to keep in mind that to "own" something, you must usually "pay" something. These are often your resources, such as time, energy, or money. At one level, a "free person" can say, "I'm going to do whatever I want!" But there is a difference between freedom and license. I suspect that most people reading this book also feel an obligation to be responsible.

If your expectations are not met in owNership, anger might be the result. You can start to feel helpless, and anxiety and anger can set in. If you have anarchy in your resource management – that is, if you fail to plan enough – you might soon find that the tyranny of urgency will fill the vacuum of anarchy. If you see this, more time might be required in the planning stage. I know that planning takes time. But often, it is needed.

1 Flood Choices. Ruthlessly clear spaces, then refill.

When my wife and I want to organize a room in our home, there are two ways we do it. The first is to look over the shelves, and remove each piece we think we no longer need. In general, this method helps a bit, but overall, it is not very effective. Our second method is to pull everything out of the room, and then re-populate it. This method works far better, with much deeper and satisfying results.

Are you currently in a situation where you see no way out? You have 300 or more unanswered emails? You have a 2 foot stack of journals? You have "to do" lists piled high? How do you manage the flood, so that you can even get back on your feet to start? How do you "drink from a fire hose", so that you can proceed with your venture?

For this exercise on "Flood Choices", I like to start with my Life Ring, which I spend time writing when separated from the flood. Then I take some area of my life – a room in my home, an email inbox, a stack of journals – and I pull all parts of it out into the open. Essentially, I empty all the items from that bucket, so that I can refill my bucket as I choose … or even dump the entire bucket![78]

Clearing the flood can be difficult. There might be significant commitments that you have with a professional organization or through a contract that would be especially difficult or irresponsible to discard next week. As one pastor told my wife and me many years ago, "If you feel like you are not doing the work you are called to do, get out! It might take 2 days; it might take two weeks; it might take two years. But start working to get out."[79] Furthermore, you might have significant emotional attachment to the area. If you are changing careers, changing homes, changing hobbies, changing churches, changing friends, changing habits … it might be hard. Emptying a bucket is not easy. You will likely have feelings like

- "I am letting my friends down."
- "I am letting the memory of that person down."
- "This souvenir meant so much to me."
- "Will I lose my identity or reputation or income?"
- "Am I leaving others behind, and leaving jobs undone?"

It is OK to mourn those losses, if you think you have a greater good ahead. Indeed, for those people who have truly cared about me, I have sometimes thought, "They might mourn with me, but in the end, I think they would agree that this is best." Give yourself permission to grieve the losses.

Exercise 14. Make ruthless Flood Choices.

For some area of your life, perhaps a room of your home, your car, your reading list, an email inbox(es), or even a career, pull everything out into the open, so that your bucket in that area is empty. At that point, use your Life Ring to guide how you re-populate the bucket ... or perhaps leave it empty. Many people find the Pareto Principle "80-20 rule" is helpful: If you keep 20% of the items, you will retain 80% of the benefit. If you are clearing your schedule, find a way to keep your most valuable 20% of effort, which will keep 80% of the benefits, and use the new-found time to try something new.

Avoid keeping items that you are doing out of habit, or because "you think you oughta because someone else thinks so", or some similar and less driving reason. Avoid that emotional guilt and perhaps even that loss in identity. These are normal feelings that you must overcome. Also avoid removing things one at a time. The key is to remove everything first, then to repopulate. This process might take 2 days, or it might take 2 years. You might hire a dumpster, or you might use a process like Fly Lady[80].

Start today. How often to do the emptying process? I find it helpful to find something each semester that I will empty and re-populate. And it requires constant vigilance! If you clear a space and don't fill it with some greater good, you can bet that some lesser good will fill the space. You might even be worse off than before!

2 Habits. Set a process for growing good habits.

In his book *Can I Have 5 Minutes of Your Time?*, Hal Becker talks about the power of the first 15 minutes of your day. When you wake up for the day, and go to sleep for the day, those are transition points that have the power to shape the rest of your day!

This is a place to have a routine to energize quickly in the morning – perhaps with some brief exercises and a cup of coffee, or perhaps time for prayer or meditation – and a routine to calm down at the end of a day – perhaps with a bowl of cereal and 15 minutes of reading. Whatever your routine, make it consistent, and if you find you are not energized in the morning and relaxed as you go to sleep, change your routine. My friend Erik Foley-Defiore told me that at the end of his work day, he says to himself, "I am done. I have done enough." I have found this to be a useful technique, and so when I get started in the morning, I say, "I start." When I finish work, I say, "I am finished." When I go to bed, I say, "I sleep."

There are other habits that we would like to build – maybe exercise, or doing your checkbook, or having a weekly lunch with your spouse. And there are also habits that you would like to stop – maybe smoking, over-eating or over-drinking, or jumping to your email box too often during the day. In *The Power of Habit*, author Charles Duhigg says that 40% of our life consists of habits. How can we change them? He describes three steps. Let's relate these to trying to develop the habit of running in the morning.

1. **cue.** If your running shoes are next to your bed, you are more likely to run when you get up in the morning.
2. **routine.** If you know your jogging path and feel safe on it, and run through a nice park, you are more likely to jog.
3. **reward.** It can be anything that says, "Good job!" You might keep a laundry basket of sweaty running clothes for the week, so that the more full it gets, the better you feel!

Exercise 15. List 3 Habits that you want to grow or drop.

Make a list of 3 habits that you want to grow, and 3 that you want to dump. Work on one at a time, and stay with it for 30 days,

until you have habitized it. If you find it difficult to continue the
habit, look for what piece is missing: a clear cue that reminds you to
do your habit today, a routine that is no less pleasant than it needs to
be, and a reward that says, "Good job!".

Perhaps most especially, define what the morning wakeup will
look like, perhaps with prayer and coffee or meditation. I know that
with myself and many of my acquaintances, we find morning
exercise an essential part of getting moving on the day. Define also
your go-to-sleep bedtime routine, perhaps with cereal or bedtime
reading. I also find it helpful to keep the times relatively fixed,
although that is not always possible for a variety of reasons.

3 Big Rock Choices. Earn the right … and choose!

Stephen Covey's story about the "big rocks" is well-known.[81]
In brief, a teacher shows her students a container, and fills the
container with fist-sized rocks. She asks, "Is the container full?"
The students answer, "Yes!" Then the teacher pours in sand. "Is
the container full?" Now the students are wiser, and answer no.
Then the teacher pours in water and declares that the container is
full. She asks, "What is the lesson?" One bright student responds,
"You can always fit a little more in the bucket!" The teacher
responds, "No. The lesson is that unless you put the big rocks in
first, they will never fit."

What are your "big rock" choices? Typically, you can only
include 2 or 3 each week. In my case, I start with my Life Ring,
which has my primary driving force on it. Then at the end of each
semester – December for the Fall semester, April for the Spring
semester, and August for the Summer session – I consider my 2 or
maybe 3 most important goals for the coming semester. This is for
self, family, venture, day job, and community. Then each week, I
place the most important tasks – the "big rocks" – that will lead
toward the semester goals. That is, I put the goals in a hierarchy, to

make them more manageable. As hard as it is, we must reduce the to-do list, and increase the to-stop list. We have the power to make these choices. Do you believe that?

Some of you are thinking, "Oh, you don't know my schedule! I have two kids ages 2 and 4, and life is a whirlwind!" Are they your priority? If so, make choices for them. "Yes, but I also need to work to support our family. Plus I am involved in community service, my church, a book club ..." You are likely over-extended. Choose 2 or 3 big rocks. You cannot choose 20 big rocks. You might be saying, "My competitors are all choosing 10 big rocks! They can do it! Why can't I?" I suspect you are not seeing their full picture.

There are at least two barriers to choosing. One is that we accumulate "to do's" and stuff over time, and these start to consume our resources of time, energy, and money. That is, we start feeling overwhelmed. I remember hearing when I was a boy, "When you get older, get the biggest shell of a house you can, so that you have a place to put your stuff." It is often a trap! It is often helpful to simplify your life as much as possible.[82] One way to simplify your choices is to appreciate that you have 168 hours per week – that is a lot of time! – and then to categorize your potential "to do's" into ABC level goals for body-mind-heart-soul. Then sub-prioritize them 123 for the A level goals. Choose the A1 rocks first, then the A2 rocks, and so on.[83]

A second barrier is that you have not yet earned the right to choose. You have not built up enough slack resources in time, energy, money, and expectations. Perhaps you would like to work at home 3 days per week. Have you convinced your employer that you are capable of doing it responsibly? Perhaps you would like to do a project with someone in the community. Have you convinced the person that you are the right helper? Have you saved enough money to do the project? My children would like to watch television whenever they want. Have they convinced me that they have done their chores and their growth exercises, and taken charge of them, so that I feel comfortable letting them watch TV whenever they choose? Building slack resources is another tool, which we will discuss next.

Tool 16. At the beginning of each week, make Big Rock Choices.

Base your top 2 or 3 choices on your Character – and especially your Life Ring. Do not choose your top 10 or 20 goals, since that is not really making a choice at all. Each big rock might take 3 to 8 hours, or sometimes more. Sometimes the goal will be to do part of a larger project. Place those "big rocks" in your calendar first thing! And avoid letting anything move them out. If you do take a "wrong turn" during the week, and get off track from your Big Rock Choices, then you can re-calculate how to get back on track, just like your GPS in your car gets you back on the right path. Don't worry yet about "how" you will accomplish your choice – you will give your "agents" permission to handle that, in a later exercise.

4 Slack Resources. Bank enough to allow adjustment.

In your endeavors it's helpful to set a "slack account" for time, energy, and money. Slack resources allow the inertia or buffering needed to make advances in other areas of your life. If you have a surge of work, you can adjust the work for the coming weeks, backing off, so that you don't get swamped. If you're last minute on every item, then when any disruption hits, it's like having no money in your bank account. For example, at holiday time, many people spend considerable time making additional food, sometimes purchasing gifts, having more guests. Do you try to finish other tasks before you get to the holidays, so that you have slack accounts to handle the surge? For example, can you do some of the holiday baking and cooking ahead of time, building slack in your system by storing food in the refrigerator, so that you can go through the holidays with less crisis?

Slack resources give you "the right" to make certain choices, in many cases, by giving you the ability to exploit new opportunities. There is an optimal between working hard, and having open slack for new opportunities. It is often difficult to advance until you're above some threshold. That is why a 50 h work week is beneficial for a career. If your job requires 40 hours per week, working 50 hours gives 10 hour to have as extra, which you can use how you see best to advance. Conversely, if your children are young or not on their own – you might especially need that time with your family.

One way to dissipate your slack resources away is to spend resources – time, energy, money – making choices outside of your "circle of influence", as Stephen Covey calls it in *7 Habits*. We have a circle of concern for things that we wish would happen, but if we lack any influence, either direct or sometimes even indirect, then that area is not in our circle of influence. Sometimes our circle of concern might be bigger than our circle of influence, such as when we are just starting out in life in a new venture, and sometimes our circle of concern might be smaller than our circle of influence, for example with retirees. When necessary, we might want to gain the right to make choices in that area, and so some work might be needed in Entrepreneurship. But until that happens, we have not earned that right.

Exercise 17. *Build savings accounts for Slack Resources.*

Build a reserve of resources in your time, energy, or money. Even a small amount of slack resources can be extremely helpful in expanding your possible choices. Find ways to build savings accounts for each of your resources.

5 Execution. Let "agents" hustle for your choices.

When our daughters were born, our lives were super-full. I was an assistant professor, still working for tenure and then promotion, and we had many new jobs that we had no idea how to handle. And yet, we still wanted a mowed lawn and a clean home. We hired agents to help us with these jobs, and it made a huge difference!

Perhaps for you there might be that there are other barriers happening in your life – even for a season – that make it difficult to execute your choices. You might have to take care of a sick child or parent; you might have a sudden deadline at work; you might have to sign up quickly for the science camp for your child. Whatever your choice, you might need to hustle to make it happen, or you might lose the opportunity. Joe Paterno used to tell his players, "Hustle, kid. Hustle. Something good will always happen if you only hustle."

Sometimes we are in a position to hire external agents to help us: doctors, lawyers, accountants, trainers, music teachers, house keepers, staff assistants, and others. Make sure they are hustling tirelessly for your choices – that is why you pay them! If they are too "relaxed", find a new person. Other times, we cannot afford such a person, or we must be without them for a season. In those cases, you are your own "agent". You might not be able to hire a sports trainer, perhaps because you cannot afford one, perhaps because you do not have time to screen for a good one. In that case you must become your own sports trainer. What does that mean? It means that you must separate your choices, from their execution. First you put on your "Big Rock Choices" hat, based on your "Character", and then separately, you find a way to hustle and make them happen. Two steps. We often delay making decisions or choices, because we are thinking about how we are going to execute the choices. In that case, we are letting our "agents" tell us how to make our choices! First choose, then execute.

When my students at Penn State take my courses, I tell them that they can for the most part choose what grade they will earn in my course. They sometimes ask excitedly, "Really? You'll let us do that?" I respond, "Sure! Here's how you do it. If you choose to earn an 'A', then spend 12 hours per week including class time. If you choose a 'B', then spend 9 hours per week. And so on." They get the idea quickly. It doesn't always work out so neatly – I know there are some students who spend 6 hours per week, and get an 'A', and some who spend 12 hours per week, and get a 'C'. But on average, the more time the students spend, the higher their grade. I know that some students are limited at earning very high grades, since they have to work to pay their way through school. Others are limited because they already have a family. Each person must make their own choices, based on their own situation.

You might ask, "What if something comes up, or if someone asks me to buy or do or consider something?" I use an automatic check valve on these decisions. I let the person know that I need to discuss the decision with my agent – maybe my accountant, maybe my wife, maybe myself – and then I can get back to him or her. I myself am responsible for the choices; my agents are responsible for the execution. It might be difficult to figure out how to execute your choices. Let your agents figure that out – even if you are your own agent. Keep your agents separate from your choices.

Making your Big Rock Choices is a proactive decision. You state your alternatives and make and design[84] your choices before you act. Execution and hustle are matter of discipline. You do those to take action. Accountability is checking up on your agent – whether the agent is hired, or yourself – which means having period meetings with them and auditing what they are doing.[85] You do that after the action. That is, you are *proactive* before, *disciplined* during, and *accountable* after execution.

Don't join the "Ain't It Awful Club"! These are the people who sit by and lament all the terrible things that have happened. As Tony Dungy, the NFL Super Bowl winning coach says, "No excuses, no explanations."[86]   One of the deans in my college wrote to the students once, "If you wait until the end of the semester to see me, I won't be able to do anything for you except get you a box of Klenex."[87]

Some people set "SMART goals".[88] SMART stands for ...

S = specific. The more specific, the better.

M = measurable. Quantitative goals are best, when possible.

A = attainable. Don't set goals beyond what can be achieved.

R = relevant. This relates to your Character and choices.

T = time-bound. Set clear timelines for your goals. Goals with dates.

As a former PhD student of mine, Joe Jones, says, "The hardest thing is moving from 0 to 1 – taking the first step." Start now! Plant seeds now!

One of the greatest business persons of all time, Milton Hershey of Hershey Chocolate fame, had a manager Frederick Winslow Taylor[89] who did "scientific management". He used organized tasks, rather than relying on initiative alone, and he had a plan for taking the first step. Why did Milton Hershey "farm out" his work? Doesn't it seem ironic to hire out your owNership tasks? Not at all! Again, the key to owNership is to 1) make your choices, 2) externalize the execution and systems to trusted external agents. The agents need to build your trust – monthly reports, accounting statements – even if the agent is you.

calendar. Have your agent position the big rocks on your calendar.

The person with the officially oldest recorded age is Jeanne Louise Calment, a French woman who lived to just over 122 years old.[90] She lived 24 hours per day. She could not slow it down, nor speed it up. "Time and tide wait for no man." You cannot store time. It marches on. This is true for the richest person on earth, like the pauper, like the super-centenarian, like the baby.

How can you control your own time? In my own case, my family calls on me, my students, my church, my professional colleagues around the world, other friends, and more. One possibility is to follow the example of the President of the United States: Have your "Chief of Staff" schedule your time. You might be your own Chief of Staff! The first thing you need to do is to follow the Stephen Covey rule: place your big rocks in the week, first thing. Typically, I find that I can place 2 or 3 big rocks in a given week. These are items that might take 3 to 8 hours to accomplish. Place them on your calendar, and avoid allowing them to move. If you have 2 big rocks per week, for 50 weeks per year, that is 100 big rocks per year. If you accomplish 100 big rocks per year, that is an extraordinary year! Measure time not by "chronos" – minutes and hours – but by "kairos" – significant moments or opportune times. What will be your 2 or 3 big rock moments in the coming week?

One way to do this is to make appointments with one of the most important people you know on earth: Yourself! Set an appointment to write for 4 hours on Thursday afternoon, or an appointment at the gym to work out, or an appointment to read a book to enjoy and revitalize. Set a Friday lunch "appointment" with your spouse for a weekly date, and if someone asks if they can see you at 12:30 Friday, you can look at them and say, "I'm sorry, we'll need to choose another time. I have a very important meeting during that time." As the book *The Power of a Positive No* describes,[91] you are filling you time with your biggest rocks, your biggest "Yes's", so that you can so "No" to other request that will otherwise inevitably take that time. Appointments with yourself, for those things that are your highest priority Big Rock Choices, are the last ones you should allow to break.

energy. Have an agent as your physical trainer, and counselor.

My friend Matt Ceglie is a personal trainer. He works with clients who often know the best way to handle their exercise, food intake, drink intake, sleep, and other health factors ... but do not have the willpower to do it. If you have willpower, be your own "personal trainer", keeping the records and holding the discipline. If not, you might need to externalize the agent, by hiring a trainer, or "hiring" your spouse or a friend or a group of friends, in order to keep you in line. Set it up! Do not delay.

If you are experiencing anxiety or other mental or emotional difficulties, you might need to externalize the agent, by seeing a licensed psychologist or counselor. For simple issues, I often find it valuable to write down my thoughts, both the facts and the feelings, and how these affect my identity. For me, there is something about seeing the words on paper or the screen, that enables me to look at them more objectively.

When my Dad wanted to lose 80 pounds back in the mid-1990s, he and Mom went to Weight Watchers. My Dad knew that he should exercise more and eat less. But he paid Weight Watchers as an agent to help him with the discipline. For many years, Dad and Mom served as their own agents for physical fitness. After about 10 years, they found they were again having some difficulty maintaining their weight, and they re-joined Weight Watchers. If you find you are not acting, identify the flaw in your plan, or find the barrier to action (TV, drugs, depression). Daily exercise provides a springboard for every other activity. I find that when I exercise first thing in the morning, my day almost always goes better.

Keep track of your numbers, as you do for all your executive positions. You can keep track of "lag" numbers, which answer, "Did I succeed?" For example, if you are trying to lose weight, your lag number is probably your bodyweight. You will also want to keep track of your "lead" metrics**Error! Bookmark not defined.**, which answer, "How do I know if I will succeed?" Two important ones for weight loss are, "How much exercise will I get each day this week?" and "How many calories am I eating this week?"

budget. Budget for today's funds, but plan for double income.

Buying on impulse is one of the greatest challenges we have. In our household, we have a rule: Do not buy any item that costs more than $10 in the same day. Always wait at least one day. If the items costs $100 or more, wait longer. Have you ever had a salesperson drop by and offer you an important set of books "for your children's education", that cost $100 or more? "But today is the only day you can buy them – I am not able to come back." Having the "1-day rule" will save you $100. You will seldom lose an important opportunity because you force yourself to wait a day. If your budget is tighter, make the number $2, but hold off on buying the same day. Have your "agent" hold you back. Wealth has been sometimes defined as "the number of days you can live, without having to work". If you are more frugal, you can extend this number of days considerably.

At the same time that you are thinking about being frugal with your money, ponder large-scale opportunities that might come your way. What if an opportunity arose for you to make $400,000 per year, or more? What if an opportunity arose to increase your wealth or income by a factor of 10 times? Would you be ready? One way to plant seeds for a higher income is to find ways to have multiple sources of income. Many of us have one source of income: Our job. If we lose our job, we have no income. This is a dangerous way to live! What if we created several sources of income – writing and selling books, making and selling jams and jellies, playing in a band, investing in real estate – and constantly work to expand our sources of income? Playing the lottery is not an alternative source of income, since most of us never win. Rather, what areas can you fruitfully contribute toward, so that you can start to develop new sources of income, and so that your day job then becomes one among that list?

Exercise 18. Give external agents permission to Execute choices.

Keep separate in your mind the choices you make for time, energy, and money, and the means of executing those choices. Either put on two different hats to help you do this, or explicitly hire someone to help you execute your choices. Treat the person executing the choices as an external agent, even if that person is yourself. Give full permission to the agents to hustle and make your choices happen quickly, one you make your decisions. Oftentimes we let the fact that execution is difficult, change the choices we know are best to sub-optimal decisions.

6 Systems. *Build processes to streamline 80% of work.*

One of the most astonishing revelations that has befallen me is that of systems. For many years I taught my courses at Penn State in a new way, got involved with ever-new research projects, got involved with new types of service activities at Penn State … and oftentimes felt drained. Then I read books that talked about systems. [92,93] Now, knowing for instance that I do not need to create "the next best course" from scratch, I use 80-90% of the material from my previous version of a course, which then allows me time to innovate on the last 10-20%. By trying to re-create half the course in order to make it better, I was wearing myself out, and not allowing enough time to do really great creative work in any one area. Due to the finiteness of life, the resources in our life allow us to make a finite number of choices. We must eat, sleep, do our day job. These are fixed. By systemizing the fixed areas, you open your possibilities in choosing the other areas.

Where do you need systems? Home? Perhaps you want to create a grocery list in Powerpoint, color-coded, so that you can print 10 copies for the coming weeks, and then each week circle those items you need. Work? Perhaps you need a new method of using "rules" to pull out your key emails into two or three special inboxes, so that you can make sure you read and work through the emails that are most important to you. Or perhaps you need to develop a system of workflow with the 10 people you manage, so that communications are clear and concise, and so that you do not hinder their work. Community? Perhaps you need to set breakfast times for your most treasured group of friends, so that you can meet at the local breakfast diner each Wednesday at 6:30 am.

After you innovate and create with Entrepreneurship, and you find good ideas, you move them to "systems" that work according to a standard process. Having systems is what enables your day job to provide the resources or cash flow that feed your venture, because with systems, you don't have to think as much about your day job. The systems enable you to deliver or ship on your promises, to satisfy those who are expecting you to produce in a responsible way. If you have 80-90% of your life systemized, then you will have enough slack resources to build on the other 10-20%. That gives you space to add your own personal "magic" in the 10%. If, on the other hand, you say, "That is too confining! I want to leave most of my life without defining too much in a system," that is OK – it is your choice. Just realize that it will make it harder for you to build your life toward achieving your passions and purposes.

In many ways, systems are types of formalized habits. A good habit takes 21 days to establish, and 6 months to make somewhat brainless. We need reminders for our systems and habits every few weeks at the most, and preferably every week.[94] If we do not have systems for things that we know how to do, we produce waste.[95] As Charles Duhigg describes in *The Power of Habit*, one strategy for helping to establish these habits is 1) set up cues, 2) establish the routine, and 3) set up a reward.[96] For example, if I want to read to my daughter each night at bedtime, and establish it as a habit or system, I need to have the book right by the bed at night (cue), have the bedtime and reading duration roughly set (routine), and have a reward like going to get another book when we finish (reward). If I am not willing to establish the habit, it likely will not continue for long.

What kinds of systems are available? In teaching a MOOC in 2013 for the first time, we developed a workflow system of using Google Docs, which we could all access and edit whenever we wanted. That system enabled us to work together. In working with our young girls in 2012, my wife and I developed a system of using beans to count advances in heart, mind, body, and soul. We measured the gains using 500 dry black beans – using 1 bean each day to mark for instance 15 minutes of exercise – and after we marked off 500 beans, we would as a family go on a small trip. You might use checklists[97], which we have found to be extremely valuable for our family, as well as at work and in the community.

Having systems enables you to build a "flywheel effect" that Jim Collins discusses in his book *Good to Great*. It enables accumulated gains over time, allowing you to gain momentum, and providing enough inertia to help get you through difficult times. Oftentimes a "breakthrough" occurs when your accumulated gains reach a new and noticeable level.

From time to time, it is also helpful to think about whether your current system is capable of handling a massive increase or decrease in resources. What if you lost your job? ... or, had a sudden 10× increase in income? Would you be ready?

Exercise 19. Put 80% of life into Systems, and add magic to 20%.
For the processes you know you must do with self, family, work, and community, systemize whatever parts you can, so that you can build slack resources that will better enable you to make your Big Rock Choices. Do not allow yourself to be a victim, but start now by systemizing your home – maybe with a standardized grocery list or cleaning schedule – and your work – maybe with an email handling routine.

Action Checklist

☐ **Flood Choices.** Every 3 to 6 months, pull everything "out of the bucket", put it on the floor, and put back those things that you deliberately choose. Avoid leaving everything on the shelf and pulling off the "less important items", because emotional attachment will prevent you from removing much at all.

☐ **Habits.** Establish particular routines for the first and last 15 minutes of the day. The hardest part of these two transition times can be confusion. This can be especially true at holiday times, or for families, in the summer when the kids are out of school. Build habits you want, and remove those you do not.

☐ **Big Rock Choices.** Earn the right to make choices, choose the 2 or 3 most important items in the entire week, and schedule them on your calendar first thing. Give plenty of time, including some "slack time". You will not finish everything you would like to – that is inevitable – but you will have a better possibility of finishing the most important items.

☐ **Slack Resources.** Build bank accounts of some resources, including money of course, but also time and energy. Avoid scheduling every second of every day – or at least have enough flexibility that priorities can be changed.

☐ **Execution.** Once you have your choices, externalize them. If you have hired assistants for your calendar, finances, or physical fitness, make sure they hustle and do their work. If you are the "external agent", treat that part of your brain as if you are your own servant, executing the choices of the "master".

☐ **Systems.** After you have a process figured out, systemize it. Make the steps crystal clear, and follow them. Your life systems are what enables you to do your "day job" efficiently enough that you can advance with ventures.

Here are some suggested additional readings:

- Covey, Stephen. *7 Habits of Highly Effective People.* (1989).
- Duhigg, Charles. The Power of Habit: Why We Do What We Do in Life and Business. (2012).
- Ferriss, Timothy. *The 4-Hour Work Week.* (2007).
- Frankl, Victor, *Man's Search for Meaning.* (1946).
- Franklin, Benjamin. *The Autobiography of Benjamin Franklin.* (1793, published after his death).

Tenacity

Once a task is first begun
Do not leave it 'til it's done.
Be the labor large or small.
Do it well, or not at all.
– Grandma Velegol[98]

Illegitimum non carborundum. – Ten
Thousand Men of Harvard, one of Harvard
University's fight songs. It means loosely,
"Don't let the bastards grind you down."[99]

Tenacity. I will hold on in pursuing my vision of _____, amidst all obstacles.

"My most difficult day in business happened over 41 years ago. It was the Valentine's Day Massacre on February 14, 1972." My friend Brian Cunningham, is CEO of the Wave Energy Conversion Corporation of America (WECCA), and founder and former CEO of Computer Entry Systems. Brian has been a very successful entrepreneur for several decades … and has learned a few lessons about Tenacity, as he describes in his book *Never Give Up*.

"I had a company called Computer Entry Systems, which had 180 associates. I personally had played a key role in recruiting and hiring them. We were in a battle with dominant players – IBM, NCR, Unisys – and in order to compete, we had to reduce labor and improve performance. On that day we had to let go of 140 of our 180 Associates. It was awful. Awful! But we didn't give up! We were Tenacious, and we stuck it out. We identified a 'key differentiator' to take on the competition, improved performance and accuracy of our company, and sped the transfer and flow of funds within our company. We stuck it out, did the work, and we won the day! Computer Entry Systems was an enormously successful company, eventually employing over 1000 Associates."

I asked Brian, "What is so hard about sticking it out? What are the key challenges?" He replied, "There are a number of challenges, including 1) feeling like a failure! Who likes that feeling? You have to overcome that emotional blow. 2) Cash flow. We found ourselves $2 million in debt! This is a genuine and tangible challenge."

"But there are also some strategies to never giving up. First, have someone to love, or at least people around you who believe in you no matter what. That is critical. Second, keep focused on your plan. Develop that strategic plan in a calm time – Darrell, you have seen my "Life Ring", and some of my strategic plans for WECCA – develop that strategic plan, and let it stabilize you during stormy times. And third, so that you do not flounder, have a battle plan with a "next step" – something to do the next morning. Those are three pieces a person needs in order to never give up, as Winston Churchill would say."

Those three pieces are indeed key to Tenacity. In this chapter I will expand upon these pieces, and describe some critical tools of how to hold on to a great hope, amidst obstacles, disappointments, setbacks, battles, discouragements, delays, drudgery, hardship, or boredom … and to finish strong. Of all the pieces that will help you hold on with Tenacity, it is having a strong Character. The more firmly-established you have in your mind what you will live for and what you will die for – the "master in the middle", or driving force of your Life Ring – the better you will be able to stick with something.

In the Velegol dining room, we have a framed print of the famous painting *Washington Crossing the Delaware* by Emanuel

Gottlieb Leutze. It reminds us to be tenacious. In some ways there were two "declarations of independence", the first declared and approved in writing on 1776 July 04, and the second committed physically and fought for by Washington's army on 1776 December 25 night. More than anyone, General George Washington never lost sight of the vision that was driving the Revolutionary War. It gave him Tenacity.[100,101]

As Seth Godin's book *The Dip* describes, the key is to know when not to give up, and when to move on quickly. The purpose of this chapter is to identify the difference, and to figure out how to "stick with it" for those areas you choose.

1 Voices. Beware the croakers. Embrace believers.

Benjamin Franklin said in his autobiography, "There are croakers in every country, always boding its ruin." You are not smart enough. You are not strong enough. You do not have enough resources. You do not have the right connections. Do you ever hear these types of statements? And do you know who is sometimes the loudest crier of these statements? Yourself! Do not believe it! Hit the "delete button" on these thoughts! You need to have the right voices whispering in your ear, based on your Courage Mirror. "I am enough. I will not be daunted by or intimidated by difficulty, danger, disappointment. The world is looking out for my best interests." Does your Courage Mirror (from the "Character" tool) say this to you?

Tenacity has many names: persistence, perseverance, grit, stamina, toughness, stick-with-it-ness, resilience, determination, hardiness, hope. Churchill said, "Never give up!' Fortune favors the deluded, and so "If you can survive, you can thrive!" Beware the voices that say to you, "The world is out to get you!" We all know people who have mastered the skill of criticism, or perfected the art of doubt! President George H.W. Bush once wrote,[102] "Sometimes in life you have to act as you think best. You can't compromise, you can't give in ... even if your critics are loud and numerous." One key, as both my friends Jack Matson and Brian Cunningham[103] say, is to find people who will believe in you no matter what. Find encouraging people, of like spirit, who will believe deeply in what you are doing.

There are also more formal methods of controlling the voice, found in the study of positive psychology.[104] For example, in resilience training[105], one examines the "me-always-everything" trio of voices.   These say, "The problem is with me, not my environment," "This situation always occurs, not just sometimes," and "Everything I do is screwed up, not just one thing!"[106] There is also a valuable "ABC concept": Oftentimes we jump from experiencing some adversity (A) in our lives, to fearing awful consequences (C), without recognizing that between A and C is B, our beliefs. As we examine those beliefs more clearly, we often find that our imagined consequences are quite exaggerated and unlikely. In some ways this is Victor Frankl's concept all over again, recognizing that between stimulus and response is a gap, which is where our freedom lies. Resilience training helps us to place truer thoughts in that gap, reducing fear ... and reducing "the voices".

We must be aware that there are times when "the voices" will have truth in them. The key is not simply to reject all negative input, but to discern what is true and helpful feedback, from what is simply negative and vague feedback. The latter is pure discouragement; reject it.   The former can provide guidance into ways of improvement.

Exercise 20. Identify positive and negative Voices in your life.
Identify the voices that are speaking most loudly too you. If they believe in you and are positive ... good! For those voices that

are negative – whether these croakers are a parent, a friend, a family member, a colleague, yourself, or others – write down their statements. Ponder whether the statement is true or not, and then determine the beliefs that you hold, which support whether you think the statement is true. Sometimes the act of writing down these pieces can slow down our minds enough that we distinguish more clearly statements given by believers, from statements given by croakers. Don't let the croakers grind you down!

2 Willpower Tunnel. Enter a path with periodic gates.

In 1963 the student who finished first in the class in the Mechanical Engineering Department at West Virginia University was Charles Vest. Later he became Dr. Vest, and rose through the ranks to eventually become a very highly respected President of MIT in Boston, and later, the President of the National Academy of Engineering. But here is a question that has been of great interest to me for many years: Who was #2 in that ME class of 1963 at WVU?

It turns out that this student went to Follansbee High School in Northern West Virginia. His father owned coal mines, and this student would often, after school, return home and load a couple tons of coal. Over time, #2 decided he didn't like loading coal, and he chose to attend college at WVU. In his first semester at WVU, he studied and worked ... and earned a 1.6 GPA! But he persisted – he still didn't want to load coal for a living. He studied harder. He chose a strong student for a roommate. He devoted more energy to his studies, because now he was on a path to a 4-year degree. And in short, that is how Dave Velegol, Sr. – I call him Dad, or David Velegol Sr. – finished second in his class.

In what areas do you need to enter a tunnel in order to accomplish your vision? Losing or gaining weight? Advancing a relationship? Learning piano? Improving your 5k running time?

Learning calculus? Starting a business[107]? For many of these, we can enter a "tunnel". For relationships, many people get married, which provides a significant barrier to leaving the relationship when times are tough. For learning calculus, many people sign up for a course and pay tuition, which provides a significant barrier to quitting, which lasts one semester. You set up these tunnels in sane moments of life, so that when difficulty arises, you cannot flee too quickly.

Sometimes your Character is so strong about some area that you might indeed want to enter a "point of no return".[108] Many world-changers from history have made such decisions, often for causes of justice or faith. However, for most areas of life, you will want to arrange periodic gates where you can exit the tunnel. At those junctures, you evaluate whether to continue in the tunnel or not. For example, if you are training for a 10k race, you might join with a group of friends, and arrange that if any of you quit training in the first three weeks, you will contribute $100 to a charity of the group's choice. After three weeks, you can decide, perhaps over a weekend period, whether to continue training, and then if you decide yes, you enter back into the "$100 tunnel" until the race. The penalty for quitting might not break you, but still it might provide enough incentive to stay in the training with your friends. And the tunnel provides a way out, if for instance other obligations overtake your time. Sometimes the tunnel will be longer, or of a different type. Here are some other types of tunnels, with examples.

- yearly or monthly. For a college degree, you enter a four or five year program, and you might decide at the end of each Spring semester whether you will change your major or not.
- number of rejections or failures. For trying to publish an article, you might commit to submitting it to 10 different

magazines or journals – facing rejection after rejection – before giving up on it.

- partners. This could be a gym partner[109], a reading partner, or a survivor partner. Every year Penn State Ladies basketball has a "Pink Game", in which they celebrate hundreds of survivors of breast cancer, in addition to remembering the fallen heroes.[110]

- deadlines. You can enter a contest for instance, in which everyone must compete at the same time.

- time commitment. Some people enter into a 30 or 40 day challenge. Many want to learn responsibility or toughness, and so they entered the military, where they had to sign onto a multi-year commitment.

- reputation. If you are on a public stage, your reputation might keep your Tenacity going.[111] Another possibility is to make a commitment in front of others, sign it across the back of an envelope, and mail it to yourself or someone else to open on a future date.

For some visions, you might care enough … that you have no exit strategy from the tunnel – a point of no return.[112] As Martin Luther King Jr. once said,

> … *you'll develop the inner conviction that there are some things so dear, some things so precious, some things so eternally true, that they are worth dying for. And I submit to you that if a man has not discovered something that he will die for, he isn't fit to live.* – Martin Luther King Jr. (Speech at the Great March on Detroit, 23 June 1963)

There is one more point I want to bring out. There are times that we find a way to "sneak out" of a tunnel. For example, let's say that you are on a diet, and you have a "black and white goal"[113] not to eat any potato chips. One weekend afternoon, a friend brings a bag of potato chips to watch the baseball game with you. You have two or three chips, and then at some point you say, "Oh, whatever!" and you eat half the bag! Having some of the mechanisms listed previously – for example, a partner in losing weight – can help get you back on track. Just as my GPS helps me get back on the path to my destination, even when I get off course, having good mechanisms for Tenacity can help you get back on track when you "sneak out of the tunnel".

Exercise 21. Take your vision into a Willpower Tunnel with gates.

One way to build willpower is to 1) have a vision for what you want to achieve to experience, 2) enter a tunnel – some arrangement that commits your time, energy, money, reputation – that holds you into the effort for a length of time, so that you don't exit whimsically, and 3) have periodic gates in the tunnel to exit.

3 Battle Plan. *Manage resistance, then pursue step 1.*

In 2008 I wanted to post one of my courses online, my ChE 350: Heat Transfer course. And I wanted to offer the course entirely online. At our faculty meeting, I got major resistance! Some faculty thought the quality would be awful. Some thought the students would hate it. Some thought this was the path to them losing their jobs. Any of these could have been true – and I am thankful that my department head helped me to manage this resistance.

Based on the resistance I received, I quickly decided to teach the course both ways that semester, online and live. As it turns out, most of the resistance was unfounded; however, some turned out to be very useful. For example, I found that while most of the students greatly preferred the online versions of the course – since the lectures could be watched whenever they wanted, and the lectures could be watched over again if wanted – about one third preferred the live version, and doing it both ways was helpful, especially in the early days of doing this. Since then, I have put several courses online, including a MOOC in "Creativity, Innovation, and Change" with over 100,000 students enrolled.

I believe in online education enough – especially for fairly standard material – that I was ready to compete and battle for it. That is the first aspect of a battle: Are you ready to sacrifice and fight for the vision? Having a clear and firm Life Ring in your Character is essential here. If you are going to have great victories, usually you will have great adversity. In fact, adversity often creates the very opportunities that we most want! And so it pays to expect battle or competition – just embrace it as a walking companion from the start – and to prepare for it, knowing the most important potential battlefronts. Will Smith, the famous actor, recommends preparing in life by "running and reading"[114]: running, so you learn never to stop (Tenacity), and reading, so you learn about any problem you have in this world (Excellence). As my Dad often says, "Rough seas make good sailors."

How to conduct the battle, when it comes? How will you manage the resistance, or as one psychologist friend of mine says, "Honor the resistance"? First, engage it swiftly. You could a) throw up your hands, b) do it all and burn out, or c) take one step at a time. Get started at winning the battle right away – peacefully if possible. You need to know the next step in pursuing your vision, and go get it. Second, avoid taking yourself "out of the game".[115]

Exercise 22. Create a Battle Plan, and when required, use it!

For any great vision, expect adversity and danger. The greater the victory, the greater the adversity, and the harder you must battle!

List the foremost potential battlefronts and temptation scenarios – enemies, drudgery, boredom, fatigue, vagueness, perhaps even violence – and prepare for them. You'll have enough battles that you don't expect, that you want to prepare for battles you do expect.

And list the very next step, which is Step 1. When you see the battle form, run to win it right away, peacefully if possible. As Brian Cunningham said, three keys to Tenacity are 1) Having someone to believe in you (Voices exercise), 2) keeping your vision clearly in mind (Willpower Tunnel), and 3) knowing your next step (Battle Plan). I once read a sign at a beach that summarized things in a similar way: "Happiness: Someone to believe in you. A dream tonight. A place to start tomorrow."

4 Transitions. Clarify expectations and adapt quickly.

We often fail at sticking with it during points of transition. I have heard it said, "By your entrances and your exits will they know you." There are two common challenges with having Tenacity during transitions: 1) expectations are not clear, which can sometimes produce fear, or at other times, draw anger by allowing implicit expectations that are not met. 2) Sometimes having Tenacity does not involve "having a thick skin", but rather, being able to disintegrate back to zero,[116] and then reintegrate quickly, and sometimes repeating this.

I love the poem "If" by Rudyard Kipling, one of my Dad's favorite poems, which he read to me as a boy when I was having difficulty during a transition:

If you can keep your head when all about you
Are losing theirs and blaming it on you,
If you can trust yourself when all men doubt you
But make allowance for their doubting too,
If you can wait and not be tired by waiting,

Or being lied about, don't deal in lies,
Or being hated, don't give way to hating,
And yet don't look too good, nor talk too wise:

If you can dream--and not make dreams your master,
If you can think--and not make thoughts your aim;
If you can meet with Triumph and Disaster
And treat those two impostors just the same;
If you can bear to hear the truth you've spoken
Twisted by knaves to make a trap for fools,
Or watch the things you gave your life to, broken,
And stoop and build 'em up with worn-out tools:

If you can make one heap of all your winnings
And risk it all on one turn of pitch-and-toss,
And lose, and start again at your beginnings
And never breathe a word about your loss;
If you can force your heart and nerve and sinew
To serve your turn long after they are gone,
And so hold on when there is nothing in you
Except the Will which says to them: "Hold on!"

If you can talk with crowds and keep your virtue,
Or walk with kings--nor lose the common touch,
If neither foes nor loving friends can hurt you;
If all men count with you, but none too much,
If you can fill the unforgiving minute
With sixty seconds' worth of distance run,
Yours is the Earth and everything that's in it,
And--which is more--you'll be a Man, my son!

Sometimes during transitions, having traditions can be helpful. As Tevye says in *The Fiddler on the Roof*, "Traditions, traditions. Without our traditions, our lives would be as shaky as... as... as a fiddler on the roof!" Life can seem precarious amidst many interruptions, and each small event can be seen as cataclysmic. Traditions can help to stabilize this. If you don't have a tradition or process for a transition event, you can create one.

One other challenge that can happen during in transitions is that your resources might increase or decrease by a factor of ten. I might suggest that for such a radical change, you move to the next exercise on "Retreats" – get away so you have time to fathom the change.

Exercise 23. Set up processes to work through Transitions.

Identify transition points in your life: starting or ending a trip, having a child born, graduating a child from high school, getting ill, getting well, getting married, getting divorced, starting or leaving a job, getting fired, having an enormous shakeup at work,[117] going to your next meeting, taking care of a child after nap time, grieving a loss, grieving a death. If you find you are having a difficult time around the time of a particular transition, set up a process that clarifies expectations. The process might be, or become, a tradition. The process might take time – it often takes a year or more to grieve a death or significant loss. Transition periods are often times when you do not have full control of a situation, and that makes it all the more important to have appropriate expectations, and a process for working through the transition period emotionally too.

5 Retreats. Get away, learn, and re-energize.

I attend several professional conferences each year in my research and teaching fields. These conferences – for me, especially the small ones – often serve as a type of "retreat" from the battles of everyday life. I typically am able to see a number of clear talks, which provoke my thoughts, and then I take enough time for reflection, including of my own life processes. Just as in the military – or even in weightlifting! – after a battle, sometimes there is a time of retreat to allow you to re-organize, grow, re-energize … and celebrate!

I have often taken my own solo retreats, usually only a day or part of a day. In the future I plan to hold my own conferences, perhaps with 10 people, and try to do it for 2 weeks, at a lovely location. I anticipate that this will be an exercise of enormous value and benefit. I'll be able to report on this in the next round of this book ☺

Exercise 24. Take periodic Retreats for revitalization and growth.

Periodically get away to re-assess how you are handling your Tenacity. Some people take time each morning to meditate or pray, and that can be critical – it is for me. Retreats, however, are usually longer, perhaps one day, or perhaps a month or more. Take time once per quarter or once per semester to travel offsite if possible. Occasionally, you will want to do this with others, maybe 10 others, or maybe more. Set an agenda, have time for open reflection and meals, and summarize the results on one sheet of paper.

Action Checklist

- ☐ **Voices.** List the voices in your life. Characterize them as useful, discouraging, and other categories, and try to list your belief system for how you categorize them.
- ☐ **Willpower Tunnel.** Starting from your vision, enter a tunnel with known, periodic gates.
- ☐ **Battle Plan.** Establish a battle plan to any anticipated resistance. When a battle arises, move right away to win the

battle, peacefully if possible. An important key is to have Step #1 clear in your mind, so that you can act right away.

☐ **Transitions.** For important transition periods in your life, clarify the expectations in a tradition or process. Allow the time for the transition process, recognizing that you might not be in control of the situation, and that it might take time.

☐ **Retreats.** Get away from the battle periodically, to give yourself an opportunity to examine your Tenacity.

Here are some suggested additional readings:

- Cunningham, Brian, *Never Give Up: Life Lessons of a Successful Entrepreneur.* (2008).
- Godin, Seth. *The Dip: A Little Book That Teaches You When to Quit (and When to Stick).* (2007). I love how this book describes both when to stick with something, and when to quit. His "3 curves of life" is a powerful concept.
- Kipling, Rudyard. "If", one of my favorite poems.
- McFarland, Keith. *Bounce: The art of turning tough times into triumph.* (2009).
- Stanley, Andy. *Visioneering: God's Blueprint for Developing and Maintaining Vision.* (2007). The story of Nehemiah and the rebuilding of the wall is absolutely full of lessons in Tenacity.

Excellence

My heart is in the work. – Andrew Carnegie

*Today I will do what others won't, so
tomorrow I can accomplish what other's
can't. – Jerry Rice, former NFL receiver*

*Seest thou a man diligent in his business? He
shall stand before kings; he shall not stand
before mean men. – Proverbs 22:29 (used in
the Autobiography of Benjamin Franklin)*

Excellence. I commit and focus hard work on gaining skill in _____.

Herbert Simon, the 1978 Nobel Prize winner in Economics, used to say that 10 years was required to become an expert, and that an expert would learn about 50,000 "chunks" of information. Malcolm Gladwell wrote in *Outliers* that it takes about 10,000 hours to become an expert, and provides numerous examples. In my own reading of many biographies and autobiographies, I find that it often takes 15 years to become Excellent at something.

If we combine these concepts, and say that it take 10 years and 10,000 hours to become an expert knowing 50,000 chunks, that is 1000 hours per year, and 5 hours per chunk. Is there anything at which you are investing that much to become Excellent? I often ask my students in my courses how many hours they will spend studying. Currently the Chemical Engineering degree at Penn State requires 134 credits. At 15 weeks per credit, and assuming that students spend 2 hours out of class for every hour in class, that is about 6,000 hours – still less than required to become an expert! I tell my students that 100 hours gives them an introduction, which is often very useful. 1000 hours gives some competence. But 10,000 hours is where the expert lives.[118] Clearly, to become an expert requires a serious commitment, and a focus on a lot of hard work. Are you ready to delay gratification that long?

Excellence will help you to compete, and indeed, it is likely the most immediately recognizable of the CENTER practices. In fact, it is what most employers pay for. And for some, Excellence is hard to acquire over and over and over again as they age – they lack the focus, the commitment, the discipline, the intensity. They find it hard to commit the hard work over many months and years, to become Excellent.

John Wooden, the highly-successful UCLA men's basketball coach of the 1960s and 1970s, told his players, "Success is peace of mind which is a direct result of self-satisfaction in knowing you did your best to become the best you are capable of becoming."[119] Success to him was not about winning or losing – although he was one of the fiercest competitors of all – but about achieving Excellence. As my friend Joey said to me, "In the real world, good enough is not good enough. It has to be excellent. We teach kids that a C is OK, but clients don't buy a C grade." And as my friend Keith said to me, "Work hard and get the details right." You might have to narrow you niche until you can be outstanding at it, but when you do, you will become known as an exceptional person who over-delivers, and you may be rewarded for it.

Excellence requires great industriousness. How hard are you willing to work at eliminating those distractions, and staying within your circle of influence? What are you willing to give up for Excellence? Summers? TV? Sleep? As Henry Wadsworth Longfellow wrote,

Heights by great men reached and kept
Were not obtained by sudden flight
But, while their companions slept,
They were toiling upward in the night.

You win in practice, and you show it in contests. Usually to do well you will need to practice in an area of relative strength.[120] Even so, set yourself to be excited by improving the process, more than by focusing ahead to the game.

In what area are you motivated to achieve Excellence? As Daniel Pink describes in his book *Drive*, motivation happens when you have autonomy to choose (owNership), when you are able to master something (Excellence), and when you work toward a great purpose (Character).[121] These three aspects – Autonomy, Mastery, Purpose – have the acronym AMP, and Excellence is part of AMPing up your life. You might choose Excellence in your health, your accounting skills, your free throw shooting, your piano playing, your parenting, your sandwich making[122], or any other area. Let's get started.

1 Hill. Choose the hill to climb and skill to learn.

In Spring 2013, my wife and I made an important observation. Around our home, we have paintings, posters, photos, and objects that form our Courage Mirror. As described in the chapter on Character, these pieces whisper the right voices to us, leading us to Tenacity, service, our faith, and even our engineering pursuits. But one day, we noticed that all the pieces ... were of men, or gender neutral. And yet, we have two daughters, ages 8 and 10!

We decided that we would modify our breakfast routine a bit, and for the entire Summer 2013, we would talk about "Great Women" with our girls. We would show their photos, describe their struggles and accomplishments, and give a brief word about how they could follow the women discussed. OK, so there is a bit of eye rolling and groaning – they are still young girl ☺ But we persisted. It was an important hill to conquer. Will it lead them to become great women? We hope so, but we are not sure. What we were sure of, however, is that we could choose these women, and do our part to bring them to the table at breakfast.

What is your hill? Do you want to change your dinner hour? Do you want to learn differential equations? Do you want to learn how to do home budgeting? Do you want to earn a PhD? Do you want to play in the piano recital? Learning new skills is the essence of gaining Excellence. My mother-in-law, Jane Butler, was an outstanding teacher, principal, superintendent (briefly), and educational consultant in New Jersey for many years. What was her secret? Every summer, she learned a new educational skill, such as differentiated instruction[123], or assertive discipline[124], or 4MAT[125]. Magic Johnson, the famous NBA basketball player, spent his summers learning new skills. One summer he taught himself the "junior sky hook", which he used to win a game in an NBA championship game against the Boston Celtics[126] -- a game I saw on television as a boy. Building Excellence is like building what Stephen Covey calls "Production Capability" (PC) in his book *The 7 Habits*. Excellence enables you then to go out and produce: To do the work, to win the game, to master the performance.

In order to gain Excellence at any skill, you must practice delayed gratification, and avoid distractions by focusing. Furthermore, Excellence demands simplicity! You must choose one – maybe two, but preferably one – major hill to climb at a time. 10,000 hours requires focus, because life is finite. And then you must stick with climbing your Hill.

Visualize the work. Visualize the contest. Visualize the joy of becoming better and better. If it energizes you, visualize the competitors. As Covey describes in his *7 Habits*, there are two creations, one mental, and one visual. Create that mental picture of Excellence, and continue to refine it.

In order to stay focused on your Hill, you will need to pull in some of the concepts from owNership. You must make one of your Big Rock Choices the preparation required to Excel, and then make a System by planting it on your calendar daily, so that it becomes a habit. Having that Big Rock on your calendar will give you the ability to say "no" to many other things.

Excellence is different from Entrepreneurship. Excellence is about gaining particular skills, while Entrepreneurship is about exploring. There are places of overlap, but overall, Excellence focuses more on the "practical" part of improving something you are already doing, while Entrepreneurship focuses more on the "potential" part of something you are first learning and exploring.[127]

Exercise 25. *Choose to climb one big Hill.*

Choose one thing that you want to gain Excellence in, *amidst all the other things that you have already to do*. That is, seldom can you give up the rest of your life, for instance if you have a family. But commit to improve the "one thing". Write it down, and state the goal clearly. As described in the book *The 4 Disciplines of Execution*, by McChesney, Covey, and Huling, this is your WIG, or Wildly Important Goal. A good WIG says, "I will go from X, to Y, by WHEN."

2 Scoreboard. Create lag-lead metrics in your ZPD.

In February 2007 I set out to lose 25 pounds by mid-year. That was my goal. I used the point-counting methods of Weight Watchers, and exercised daily. And sure enough, within about 4 months, I had lost 25 pounds. I had done several things right, even though I didn't necessarily know it at the time.

First, I had set up a WIG, as described in the exercise on "Hill". In my case my WIG was, "I will go from overweight, to fit, by mid-year." My goal was numerical: I wanted to lose 25 pounds. This is what the authors call a "lag goal" or "lag metric". Another lag goal for me was to lose roughly one pound per week. A lag metric says, "I have been successful if I see ____." In this case the lag metric is easily measured on a bathroom scale, and the result is numerical. The idea is that we measure what we care about.

Next, I set up various daily plans, such as exercising for 30 minutes each day with vigorous running or walking, and eating fewer than 28 Weight Watchers points per day. The authors call these "lead goals" or "lead metrics". A lead metric says, "I will be successful if I ____." Lead metrics are predictive, and in some ways, they are an educated guess of what will work.[128]

I acted daily on the lead goals, and checked daily on the bathroom scale for my lag goals. This accountability process is essential. Each day or no less than each week, take 10-20 minutes to check that you and your team have accomplished your one or two lead goals that you set for yourselves that week, and periodically monitor that your lead goals are in fact predicting and leading to your lag goals. Your lead goals need to be primarily within your capability – say, 80% within your control – without overly-depending on others. The enemy of accountability is ambiguity. Write what is expected. You can also set SMART goals, as described in the "Execution" exercise under owNership.

In setting goals, it is important to work within your "zone of proximal development" (ZPD).[129] When working in the ZPD, you stretch yourself to improve, but not beyond what your capacity will stand. If you stretch too far, and do not achieve your goal, you can cop out, saying, "Oh well, it was a big goal." By staying within your

ZPD most of the time, you can improve and be accountable. Don't grab too much, like the fable about the boy and the filberts, in which a boy reaches into a jar to grab filberts, but because he grabbed too many, he couldn't pull his hand out of the jar.[130]

Having numerical metrics can also serve as an encouragement. Sometimes with Excellence, it might seem like we're pouring in effort, but cannot see the end. You don't know where the river ends, by the source. The Lost River in the Appalachian Mountains of West Virginia disappears underground and reappears as the Cacapon River.[131] But by having metrics, you can maintain a better awareness of the actual progress being made, even when it is not readily apparent to others.

Exercise 26. Keep track of progress with a Scorecard.

Identify a few lag goals – which tell you whether you have been successful – and a few lead goals – which tell you if you will be successful. Make these into numerical metrics if at all possible, and keep focused on them. And do not set too many metrics, which will confuse you and reduce y our ability execute. Act on the lead goals, and re-adjust the lead goals periodically as necessary. Always set your lead goals within your ZPD, so that they stretch you, but also so that they are realistic enough to accomplish.

Then each week – or perhaps even more often – have an accountability session where you and each member of your team tell each other how you did on the lead goals that you set for that week.

3 Coach. Set practice rituals and seek critique.

When I was Chief Engineer of the Senior Design Project at West Virginia University in 1991-1992, I held a meeting early in the second week of class. I wanted to let everyone know that we would be meeting at set times each week, and I invited them to write down any critiques they had – at that meeting, and at future meetings – on a sheet of paper. I had read to do these things in the Summer of 1991, although I don't remember where.

By the end of the 1992 academic year, one of my professors called me into his office to give me his assessment of the previous year. "I thought you were in real trouble. Already by the second week of class, you were asking how to improve. I thought for sure you were headed down the tubes. Now I know – you were just seeking critique, in order to improve." I hadn't formalized the thought in my head before he had said it, and ever since, it has stuck. I have always sought critique[132] from others – including on this book! If you see ways to improve it, please email me (see front of book), and let me know how I might improve!

As I have gone on to work with students here at Penn State, I now see even more clearly the importance of setting regular meetings and "practice rituals" – such as a formal weekly lab meeting, or formal weekly office hours, as most faculty do – and asking for periodic critique from my students. In my case I use a weekly "Opinion Box" in which students can anonymously submit what they understood that week, what was unclear, questions they have, suggestions, and any other comments, including personal questions or life questions. Sometimes you even have to pay to receive critique, as we have done on some research proposals, in which we pay colleagues a small amount to pre-review the proposal before it is reviewed by a funding agency. As a leader, you have to be coachable, open to critique by others. As Professor James (Jim) Hamilton of Penn State Mont Alto once told me, "Every semester I tell my students, 'Every person in this room knows more than me … about something.'" It is true that iron sharpens iron.

Exercise 27. Set practice habits and seek critique from a Coach.

Set regular practice rituals, including a time and location, habits that you want from participants, and expectations. Ask for critique from your coaches. If you are the one you are "coaching", you can give critique to yourself. And if you are coaching others, remember that you might need to balance tough and tender[133], often in the ratio of one critique for five encouragements.

4 Problem Solving. Process through a clear problem.

I often tell my PhD students that the most difficult part of research is asking a good question. A "good" question is one that is interesting and usually important, one that can be answered in a finite amount of time – maybe 1 week, maybe 5 years – and also one for which you can hypothesize what the answer might look like. In my own field, "How do I keep paint from clumping up when applied?" is not a good question, while "What is the charge nonuniformity on individual paint particles, in mV^2 per patch?" is more clear, answerable, and important. In your own field, your questions will look different than do mine in my research area of colloid science, and that is OK.

"What are your research questions?" is a question that I ask almost every student giving a talk, from undergrads to mid-way PhD students, because it is such a hard skill to acquire. Usually, a bigger question is too big to answer all at once, and so it must be broken down into 3 or 10 or 50 parts, until you reach questions that are manageable and can actually be answered. Then you can tackle these questions one at a time, day by day. How does one acquire the skill of asking good questions and posing important and interesting problems? With practice.

Once you have good questions, the next step is to apply a process to problem solving. Scientists and engineers are not simply "smart people" who know a lot; rather, they have learned a process that enables them to solve a wide variety of problems. Many fields have problem-solving methods,[134] which while they have some similarities, also have some domain-specific aspects, such as the historical investigation method[135]. Here I list a variant of the "scientific method", much as we "learned" it in 3rd grade:

- **vision.** Developing a clear vision usually happens prior to what we normally call the "scientific method". A clear vision is helpful to asking interesting and important questions.

- **problem statement (questions).** Ask clear questions and state clear problems. A good question is interesting, important, and answerable with finite resources (time-energy-money). Usually, you will have to break down larger questions into smaller ones.

- **background.** Get preliminary background information from experts, books, personal experience, the internet. This might take 30 minutes, or 3 days, or longer.

- **hypothesis.** Form a clear hypothesis -- what you think will happen -- and then set out to test it. As much as possible, put specific measures into your hypothesis. Measures drive action. Quantitative measures are usually the most actionable.

- **experiment.** Once you know what you need to learn, and have a guess of what to expect, design an experiment so that you can learn the result. It might be a survey, a taste test, a fabricated experiment, or some other test.

- **prototypes.** This step is more common in engineering, and is like running an experiment. Build a "minimal viable product" (MVP) for the audience you intend to address. Oftentimes it will not work! You want to build it so that you can learn what you need to learn, and measure what you need to measure.

- **results.** Once you have the results from your measurements, you might find that you need to iterate, and perhaps form a new question, or perhaps keep your question and form a new MVP. The feedback process is critical.

- **action.** The last step is to take action, which will often mean to iterate again, perhaps refining the questions, perhaps forming a new hypothesis, perhaps forming a new experiment or prototype.

Just as with Intelligent Fast Failure, you can expect some early flops, but that's OK! You want to make failures that are early-small-fast-cheap, as opposed to late-large-slow-expensive. Most commonly, you will need to conduct iterations. For example, after you obtain your first results in a learning cycle, you might decide, "That question was not quite clear enough. I need to refine, because the answer is confusing two different concepts." And then you iterate.

Exercise 28. Practice the Problem Solving method.

Choose 2 critical questions you need to answer for a venture on which you are working. Refine the questions by asking others, and work through a problem solving method like the scientific method that we all "learned" in 3rd grade. Establishing an interesting, important, and answerable question is often the hardest part of this process.

5 Reading. *Read many books you love.*

Before the age of 30, I seldom read books that were not science or engineering related. For Christmas 2000, my wife gave me two books that forever changed that, by and about President Ronald Reagan. Since then, my reading has increased dramatically. Over the last 5 years, I have been reading about 1 book per week.[136] I have a "Velegol's top shelf" of books at home, which I occasionally read again. Reading gives me a chance to spend 30-60 minutes every day with some of the smartest and most interesting people in the world, to experience some of the most important and fascinating times in history, and to visit some of the most beautiful and exotic lands on earth.

How do I find time to read that many books? Actually, I don't. I download a lot of books from Audible.com, typically buying 24 credits at a time, so that each book costs about $10. Then I listen to books on my iPhone at double speed as I walk, exercise, or drive. Short books might take 2 hours; one book about George Washington by Ron Chernow took about 42 hours (actually, about 2/3 of this, or 28 hours, on "double speed"). I don't even mind sitting in traffic as much these days! At the same time, I have my little audio voice recorder, and I keep notes on the books, typing them in at the end of the day.

Why read these books? I find that for my ventures, I tend to have many questions to bring them from vision to reality, and most often, someone has written about the questions that are most pressing to me. And so I read the books that interest me most, that I just cannot put down. If a book doesn't grab my attention in the first chapter or two, I get the next book. Might I miss important reading in this way? Yes, but since the second book is likely as important as the first one, if the second is more interesting, it "wins" with me.

I still like technical books, but I have also grown to enjoy biographies and other types of non-fiction. I enjoy reading some fiction books with my daughters, and I suspect that this will increase as they grow older. There are also many books about "how to read a book" and "what types of books to read".[137]

Exercise 29. Spend time with great people, through Reading.

Get a book from the library; buy a book from the bookstore; download a book on Kindle; or sign up for an Audible account. Find a way to systemize – think back to the owNership exercise on Systems – 30 minutes of reading per day. List the first five books you plan to read next, for interest and pleasure.

Action Checklist

☐ **Hill.** Clarify what skill you intend to learn, to move toward Excellence.

☐ **Scoreboard.** Establish lag goals to answer "Was I successful?", and lead goals to answer "Will I be successful?". Numerical goals are the most actionable.

☐ **Coach.** Set times to practice the skill, avoiding unnecessary distractions and hurry, and seek critique whenever possible, including in a contest.

☐ **Problem Solving.** Answer your most important questions be taking the time to define a clear problem, breaking it down, and then answering it using a process like the scientific method.

☐ **Reading.** Choose 5 books, and systemize a way to read them.

Here are some suggested additional readings:

- Wooden, John; Carty, Jay, *Coach Wooden's Pyramid of Success: Building Blocks for a Better Life*. (2005). Note especially the systematic way that Coach Wooden worked with players. Much of his success was built on a process.
- McChesney, Chris; Covey, Sean, Huling, Jim. *The 4 Disciplines of Execution: Achieving Your Wildly Important Goals*. (2012).

Relationship

Hello, Goodbye, Thank You, I Love You,
Excuse Me, Please, I Need Help, Beg Your
Pardon, I'm sorry, Good Night, Good
Morning, I Forgive You. – "Keys to Life", in
the shape of keys on orange craft paper, done
by my Dad in class with his 1ˢᵗ grade teacher,
Ms. Warner

If you live to be a hundred, I want to live to
be a hundred minus one day, so I never have
to live without you. – Winnie the Pooh

• Don't criticize, condemn, or complain. • Give
honest and sincere appreciation. • Become genuinely
interested in other people. • Smile. • Be a good
listener. • Encourage others to talk about
themselves. • Talk in terms of the other person's
interest. • Make the other person feel important –
and do it sincerely. – selected principles from Dale
Carnegie[138]

Relationship. My family is _____; my home is _____.

I was born and raised near Pittsburgh. One of the all time great sports figures from Pittsburgh is Roberto Clemente, a perennial All Star, and the National League's Most Valuable Player Award in 1966. During his 18 years with the Pirates, he won 12 Gold Glove

Awards, and was an outstanding hitter, getting his 3000th hit at the very end of the 1972 season.[139]

Clemente was deeply involved with charity work in the Caribbean and Latin America. At one point, after a difficult earthquake in Nicaragua, he arranged for relief supplies to be sent. As supplies were being delivered, it became known that the supplies were being diverted by corrupt officials. Clemente decided to make the trip himself, hoping that his presence would help the supplies get through to the earthquake survivors, and so he joined the relief flight set for 1972 December 31, New Year's Eve. But almost immediately upon takeoff, his DC-7 airplane exploded and plummeted into the waters off of Puerto Rico. His body was never found.[140]

It was a tragic night. A former teammate and opponent of Clemente, Rudy Hernandez, was in Puerto Rico that night. He sadly recounted, "The streets were empty, the radios silent, except for news about Roberto .... All of us cried. All of us who knew him and even those who didn't wept that week."

The catcher for the Pirates, Manny Sanguillen, was one of Roberto Clemente's closest friends. Hernandez said, "Manny Sanguillen, the Pirates catcher, and (Clemente) were very close. Manny was in my joint that night. When he heard the news, he and a couple of guys jumped in their car and raced out there. They got a small boat and Manny started diving in the water to see if he could find something. There are sharks out there, man. I mean real, man-eating sharks and he didn't care."

At Clemente's memorial service, the entire Pittsburgh Pirates team attended ... except for one. Manny Sanguillen chose instead to continue in the waters, looking for his friend Roberto Clemente. As of 2013, Manny Sanguillen still goes to the Pirates games at PNC Park in Pittsburgh, where he operates Manny's BBQ behind the center field fence.

This chapter examines two of the most important questions about relationships: 1) Who is your family? 2) Where is your home? We of course have our blood relatives, but I prefer to think of family a little more broadly than that. If everything were to go wrong in my life, most people either wouldn't know about it, or wouldn't care. I might have 70 who would say, "Ahhh – what a shame!" But I also know that I have a dozen who would weep, and feel my pain. That is my family. As Jim Butcher once said, "When everything goes to hell, the people who stand by you without flinching -- they are your family." That is closer to what I am describing in this chapter. After discussing family and home, I examine a few processes that can help you start, grow, and sustain life-giving, vital relationships.

1 Family. Love and trust 3 and 12 loyally.

One of my favorite movie scenes occurs in *Blindside*, starring Sandra Bullock, in the "football practice scene".[141] The gigantic Michael Oher is in football practice, playing as if he were a 5-year-old-boy, missing blocks and being totally ineffective. The Mom, Leigh Anne Tuohy, played by Bullock, enters the practice field, pulls Michael side, and tells Michael, "This team is your family, Michael …. Are you going to protect the family, Michael?" He answers, "Yes, Ma'am." And then he proceeds to block into the next century anyone who tries to tackle "his family".

Do you have friends who will watch your "blindside"? At work? In the community? At home? Or do you have friends who will "search the waters" for you, like Sanguillen did for Clemente? It is important to distinguish between "transactional friends" and your 12. Transactional friends want to be with you – or not – because of what you have, or how you're known. "Search the waters" friends – your 3 or your 12 – are much harder to come by.

As one person once said to me, "Show me your friends, and I'll show you your future."

When I was a PhD student in Pittsburgh, I had a neighbor Ardenia Saunders, a wonderful, gregarious lady in her late 80s. Everyone knew her and loved her. One day while I was getting the mail, she and I started talking about friends. And she looked at me and said, "Darrell, if you find as many true friends in a lifetime as you can count on one hand, you are a lucky boy." I understand her words more deeply now.

How do we find these friends? Is it simply a matter of luck? Well, as we discussed earlier, there are ways to "master the luck". One of these is to sacrifice-sacrifice-sacrifice for others.[142] Go to the funeral, help with the work, stay late after work to help, send an encouraging note, be vulnerable[143], ask about their parents. And never sit by while someone else's kids are being hurt. In *The 7 Habits*, Covey discusses an "emotional bank account". Every sacrifice adds as a deposit. Every kept promise adds to the account. At other times, you might make a withdrawal from the relationship. If you and your family – again, whether they are blood relatives or other extremely close friends – if you will make deep deposits through sacrifice, you will reach a point of mutual love and trust where the loyalty account is beyond measure. You give – and receive! – spontaneous sacrifice, rather than measured sacrifice. It would be as if someone put $100 billion into your bank account. These are people you are willing to advocate and fight for. And so we see that if we want to have "search the waters" family, we need to sacrifice deeply.

Relationships magnify outcomes in life. If you are trustworthy, you get far more than you expect, and your 3 and your 12 lead you to become a "bigger you", and a better, more authentic version of yourself. They speak to you not just as you are, but also as you hope to be. On the other hand, if you abuse the relationship, you get worse

.... With transactions, you receive in proportion to what you give, and you have to watch your back. Having to do this all the time is draining and limiting, which is why it is so much better to have relationships.

In my own case, I have to catch myself so that I am not too quick to quick to disappoint my 3-12. After all, aren't they the ones who will understand, if I answer that last email, take that last phone call, visit one more student? Yes they are. And that is often precisely the challenge. Remember, most of the time, it cost the person who sent that email, or made that phone call, or asked for 5 minutes, very little, in comparison to the many years that our most cherished 3-12 have spent with us. The new person is important, but be careful not to disappoint your 3-12 too often. After all, why do we spend so much time and effort building reputations outside our 3-12? I like to think that in making sure I spend enough time with my 3-12, that I am not timid, but bold in disappointing those outside. That's hard to do, isn't it?

One way that I find useful to make sure I get focused, committed time with my wife Stephanie, is that at the beginning of each semester, we set a weekly date time. It is usually during lunch, when our girls are still in school. There is nobody on earth I would rather spend time with than her! If someone wants to meet during that time, I almost always say no – I have a more important appointment. Only occasionally do one of us ask if we can reschedule our date time, to join another meeting. I do the same thing with some guy friends, in a weekly breakfast. In fact, in making my plans for the coming semester and week, I usually try to account for how my 3-12 fit into those plans. Sometimes the people whom we can see *anytime*, end up being the people we see too *seldom*, and so we need to set up *particular* times to see them. They are too dear to take for granted.

Exercise 30. List 3, then 12, in your Family.

List 3 people, and then 12 people, whom you interact with regularly, and whom you would mutually sacrifice tremendously. The usual challenge is that it is very hard to limit your list to a small number of people, even though that is in reality whom we actually interact with. Do they have needs now, into which you can pour of yourself and deepen the relationship even further?

2 Home. Know people, resources, power structure.

Sam Rayburn was a Democratic Congressman, and Speaker of the House of Representatives of the United States for 17 years – the longest time in the history of the nation. Sam Rayburn died of pancreatic cancer in 1961, but before that, he moved back to his home in Bonham, Texas. He said, "In Bonham, Texas they know when you're sick and they care when you die." It was still home to Mr. Bayburn.

Where is your home, or your homes? Are there places where people would know when you're sick, and care when you die? Are there places where you have immersed, and know the best spots to visit, the services available, and most importantly, people who also call the area "home"? When you leave that area, will you leave a hole? If you were to die, would people say nothing, or "Oh, that's a shame?" Or would they weep?

Exercise 31. Identify the places you consider to be Home.

List places in this world where you know people well enough that you might call it "home". Do you also know the resources in the area, in terms of parks, attractions, or services? Do you also know the power structure at that location, so that you can better contribute back to the well-being of the area?

3 Rules of Civility. Write your rules to dignify others.

When he was 16 years old, future General and President George Washington wrote *Rules of Civility & Decent Behaviour In Company and Conversation*. For instance, the first two of these are "Every Action done in Company, ought to be with Some Sign of Respect, to those that are Present," and "When in Company, put not your Hands to any Part of the Body, not usually Discovered." Although Washington likely obtained these from an etiquette manual, it is interesting that he thought enough about "rules of civility" that he wrote them down! Ben Franklin and Thomas Jefferson also had lists of rules for themselves.

What are your "rules of civility"? In the quotes at the beginning of this chapter, I list the "keys to life" that Ms. Warner gave to my Dad in 1st grade. The use of these keys is a sound rule of civility, and three of most powerful phrases known are "I love you", "I am sorry", and "Thank you". Dale Carnegie had famous rules of civility, especially his 3 C rule: Do not criticize, condemn, or complain. One rule that we use in our home is that if people are not paying attention to you, don't whine; rather, make your own party, in some form.

When I was interviewing for an academic position after my PhD at a highly-regarded Ivy League school, one faculty member asked me if I wanted a cup of coffee, as we approached a coffee shop. I responded, "I don't drink coffee," and that's all I said. Awkward moment. Another rule of civility might be, "Strongly consider accepting a beverage or snack when it is offered." Rules of civility involve manners and practices that lead to dignity and respect.

Exercise 32. List your own Rules of Civility.

Your list might contain 5 items, or 25, or 125. You might include the "keys to life" in the quote for this chapter, or you making include something about shaking hands and looking someone right in the eye, or about turning off your iPhone, or about being on time. How do you want to show your respect for others?

4 Crucial Conversations. Engage hard discussions.

Have you ever had to fire someone[144]? Or let them know that they needed to find another position? Or have you ever had to tell someone, "What you're doing is not acceptable?" It's not easy. Two very good books on crucial conversations or difficult conversations are listed at the end of this chapter. For here, I want to focus on just a few points.

First, in order to have a successful conversation, you need to listen. Most of us have been hearing since we were born, but that doesn't mean we have been listening. When we listen, we need to hear the facts of the case, but we also need to hear the emotions and feelings of the other person – after all, the facts might not be the critical issue, or they might be too subtle to discern easily – and we also need to understand how the facts and the feelings impact the identity of another person.

When I was an assistant professor working toward tenure, my wife and I would have "discussions" about not spending enough time with her. Didn't she know how hard it was to get tenure? Didn't she want what was best for our family? Didn't she want me to help those students? Of course she did. She also wanted appreciation for all that she was doing, apologies for those times when I messed up, and moments when we could connect. I missed so many of those needs, because I was too focused on the obvious facts – that I needed to work hard – and her concerns also seemed to attack my identity as a faculty member. While we still work on these issues today to some extent, we have gone beyond being dogmatic in wanting to be right, and now we recognize the importance of listening to facts, feelings, and identity – a large part of being empathetic. We also recognize that conflict is unavoidable, but combat is a choice.[145]

Being empathetic, however, is different from winking at trouble. Part of our conversation with family, friends, teams, and associates is to work hard at clarifying expectations and boundaries. Don't shrink from applying standards, or applying justice. Justice tells everyone, "I care."

A second point for crucial conversations is the importance of negotiation. In *Getting to Yes*,[146] the authors describe the importance of having a BATNA, or "best alternative to a negotiated agreement". If you have a BATNA, then you have input for a negotiation. Otherwise, you will have a very difficult time. If you go to a fine restaurant on Valentine's Day night, with no reservation, your BATNA might be McDonald's because all the fine restaurants are booked. You have little control. If you go on a less popular Tuesday evening, when the restaurant has many open tables, you have the ability simply to go to another restaurant. When you have a BATNA, you will hopefully find that as you negotiate, that there are pieces valuable to you, that are less valuable to another, and vice versa, so that you can have an exchange and both come out ahead.

Exercise 33. Plan two Crucial Conversations you should engage.

The conversations could be with your spouse, your child, your friend, your co-worker. Write the difficult core of the conversation, and develop a BATNA. Write what you know about the situational facts, the other's feelings, and potential identities that the participants hold.

5 Team. *Organize with those of like interest.*

In Spring and Summer 2013, I was working with a group of about a dozen people in designing and delivering a MOOC (massive open online course) in "Creativity, Innovation, and Change" (CIC). It was the CIC MOOC. We had over 100,000 students enrolled for a launch of 2013 September 01. I spent at least 5× – and maybe 10× – as much effort as I had in preparing for any previous course I had taught, and even then, I was only part of the effort.[147] But I was absolutely energized, and the course preparations went remarkably well. I believe that our team was critical to this, and that a team of highly systemized, cooperative, "ordinary" people, will almost always out-compete a team of disorganized "outstanding" people.

In his book *The 5 Dysfunctions of a Team*,[148] Lencioni lists the following as the primary dysfunctions: 5) inattention to results (i.e., lack of owNership Execution), 4) avoidance of accountability (lack of Excellence with a Coach), 3) lack of commitment (lack of Character, or Excellence), 2) fear of conflict (lack of Relationship Crucial Conversations), and 1) absence of trust (Relationship lack of vulnerability).

What were the secrets to forming, growing, and maintaining our MOOC team?

1. **shared project.** We all wanted to build a great MOOC – a project worth fighting for – to educate students in CIC. I believe that great work led to a great team, as much as a great team led to great work. The project is the glue that holds people together, and so build great workflow systems that lead to great work!

2. **friendly people.** Even one toxic person can sabotage a work environment.   In working together, I cannot remember ever using adamant, dogmatic language. We spoke in open tones, like Benjamin Franklin would have

used. If you have such toxic person, do not hesitate to get rid of him or her! Avoid toxic people!

3. **diverse members.** As I have learned from Kathryn Jablokow, our teams in many cases require members with Creative Diversity, for example in how much structure they require, and whether their ideas are revolutionary and evolutionary. All these contributions are important.

4. **Trust[149] and loyalty.[150,151]** We all trusted the leader, Jack Matson, to the core. Jack pulled together the team, and therefore we trusted each other. We could be vulnerable with each other, and therefore we had a high level of creativity and productivity. Our trust and loyalty provided the inertia to get through some difficult times, and we were "relational" rather than transactional, inclusive rather than extractive,[152] smiling rather than harsh.

5. **accountability.** We had weekly phone meetings in which we assessed what was needed for the following week, said what part each of us would do, and then the following week, showed which part we did. It was a system of weekly accountability. As President Ronald Reagan said, "Trust but verify." It is a powerful formula for success.

6. **systems.** We allowed each other to specialize, and we used Google Docs and other methods to allow synergistic workflows. We did not fall into the "local efficiency trap", thinking that just because I am working hard, all must be going well. We watched out for each others' workflows and how they fit into the system.

Some might think that a good team produces good results. But I usually find that it is the converse: good results produce a good team. And how to produce good results? Have people with the right skills, working together, with a good system or process. Keep your focus on what glues you together, produce great results, and your relationships will go well as a team. Work can be the lubrication of relationships. After all, everyone on the team wants to be part of something great.

Exercise 34. Organize a Team with proper skills and diversity.

Identify the skill sets – both technical skills and relational skills – needed to accomplish your venture. In order to find people for your team, use your network of family and friends. In order to pre-screen candidates, I like to ask for a 2-minute YouTube video and a resume. In order to learn the relevant information about potential team members, I learn about candidates relative to a "scorecard" that I develop ahead of time. And once I have these pieces completed, and find the right person, I recruit them in with energy. These are the steps outlined in the book *Who*, by Smart and Street.

6 Power. Persevere toward the tipping point.

On 2005 October 24, Rosa Parks died. I remember the time well, because I spoke about her in my class for one of my CENTER stories, and it was with great emotion. I still have the photo from the cover of the *USA Today* on 2005 October 31, with her lying in honor in the Capitol Rotunda, with President Bush standing there. The headline read, "The Nation Pays Tribute to Rosa Parks". How did Rosa Parks have the courage to say to bus driver James F. Blake, "I don't think I should have to stand up."?

As Susan Cain wrote in her book *Quiet*,[153] Rosa Parks had been on that same bus a dozen years earlier. In the intervening time, Parks had been active in numerous learning experiences for social justice. In the Summer of 1955, just a few months before the bus incident, she attended the Highlander Folk School,[154] the adult school in Tennessee that helped activists learn about workers' rights and social justice. Rosa Parks persevered in her quest for racial justice over many years, learning strategies, gaining confidence, and then taking action. She had won power over a number of years, and used it at the right time.

What are the strategies to power? In 1982 John Gaventa wrote *Power and Powerlessness: Quiescence & Rebellion in an Appalachian Valley*.[155] He described three dimensions of power, which include a threat power, a non-issues power, and a third dimension, a perception of issues power. A few years later, the famous social scientist Kenneth E. Boulding argued in his book *Three Faces of Power*[156] that power – which he defines essentially as the ability to get what we want – is of three types: Threat power, economic power, and integrative power. Integrative power involves community relationships, including love, respect, and identity.

It is interesting to me that both authors emphasize the power of community and perceptions as being important to power. Rosa Parks had these. Many of us simply want autonomy – we want to be left alone. But as Jeffrey Pfeffer says in his book *Power*,[157] there is a tradeoff between autonomy and power, in many cases. Having power – the ability to get what we want – can come at the cost of losing autonomy. Which do you need right now, to achieve your vision, your driving force at the center of your Life Ring? If you need time to incubate your vision before rolling it out, you might need autonomy more than power. You might need to incubate your ideas, or gather resources, or rest, or learn some of the techniques for gaining power,[158,159] or learn the organization chart. But if you have a clear vision and are ready to push it forward, you might have to surrender part of your autonomy, interact more – perhaps even more than is comfortable, and exert your power. How you exert that power will depend upon your values and personality[160]; in my own case, I value having dignity for every person, and although I know I often fail, this is my preferred mode. Especially in modern times, when information flows much faster and more completely than it did centuries ago, Machiavellian techniques have lost a bit of luster.

Sometimes you will need to move swiftly if you see a battle coming. After all, the other side is likely organizing, and especially when you have authority or duty – including the duty of justice – you might need to move. And yet, I see over and over in history the truth of Martin Luther King's words: "... the arc of the moral universe is long, but it bends toward justice."

Exercise 35. *Write steps toward having Power.*

Choose the balance of autonomy and power that you need to advance your vision. If you need autonomy, use it without anxiety, growing your venture. If you need power, learn it and exert it with dignity, hopefully in a grand cause that extends far beyond yourself.

When others seek to exert power over you, assess the situation. Powerful people can work to gain power over you through intimidation and fear, through economic means, and most especially, through community methods and framing of perceptions. The person might even be a bully. Think of ways that one or two powerful people or organizations are trying to gain power over you, controlling you in ways that you do not wish, even by subtle means. Write down their techniques, and write a way that you can work around their techniques of guilt, threats, intimidation, disinformation, and other similar techniques.

7 Stones. *Mark high point moments with gratitude.*

In my family we celebrate not only birthdays, but even half birthdays! The tradition of celebrating birthdays goes back to when I was a boy: My Mom never missed making us our favorite meal, making our favorite cake, and getting us a gift. Never missed. We celebrated family victories, holidays, and so many other things. I can remember most of these vividly.

We and our friends have sometimes gathered actual light-colored stones, and written on them things we want to celebrate. Perhaps a personal victory, perhaps an improved marriage, perhaps a job promotion. And then we place them around our homes in locations where we won't miss them. It's a great way to remember those things that you choose to remember, and to give thanks for them. It is easy to lapse into a "I deserve" or entitlement mentality, and gratitude keeps this in check.

Exercise 36. *Take time to celebrate Stones.*

List 5 memories that your children, friends, or colleagues will celebrate with you, time after time over many years. What are the Stones? A birthday, an anniversary, a baptism, a promotion, a book signing, a first job, a graduation, a life decision?

Action Checklist

- ☐ **Family.** List 3 and 12 with whom you have loyal trust and energy, and whom you would sacrifice anything for.
- ☐ **Home.** List one or more locations where you know the people, attractions, and resources, so much that if you left, people would know it, and feel a hole.
- ☐ **Rules of Civility.** Write your own list of manners and other rules of civility.
- ☐ **Crucial Conversations.** Assess whether you need to have a challenging conversation with anyone, and prepare for it.
- ☐ **Team.** Recruit and organize a group of like-minded people toward a common venture.
- ☐ **Power.** Determine whether you need autonomy or power at this point, in order to advance your vision, and seek to use either with dignity.

☐ **Stones.** Establish several reasons to celebrate, and write the reasons on light-colored stones, as reminders of gratitude.

Here are some suggested additional readings:

- Carnegie, Dale. How to Win Friends and Influence People. (1936 original, 1981 revised). This book is on "Velegol's top shelf".
- Covey, Stephen, *7 Habits*. See especially Ch 05 on listening.
- Feiler, Bruce. *The Secrets of Happy Families: Improve Your Mornings, Rethink Family Dinner, Fight Smarter, Go Out and Play, and Much More.* Harper Collins, New York (2013).
- Fisher, Roger; William L. Ury and Bruce Patton. *Getting to Yes: Negotiating Agreement Without Giving In.* (1991, 2011).
- Grant, Adam M. *Give and Take: A Revolutionary Approach to Success.* (2013).
- Patterson, Kerry. *Crucial Conversations: Tools for Talking When Stakes are High.* McGraw-Hill (2012).
- Pfeffer, Jeffrey. *Power. Why some people have it – and others don't.* (2010),
- Stone, Douglas; Bruce Patton, Sheila Heen and Roger Fisher. *Difficult Conversations: How to Discuss What Matters Most.* (2010).
- Ury, William. *The Power of a Positive No: Save the Deal, Save the Relationship and Still Say No.* Bantam Books, New York (2007).

Making CENTER Practical

So never lose an opportunity of urging a practical beginning, however small, for it is wonderful how often in such matters the mustard-seed germinates and roots itself. – Florence Nightingale

The study and knowledge of the universe would somehow be lame and defective were no practical results to follow. – Marcus Tullius Cicero

Plan your week.

I use CENTER practices in every aspect of my life: self, family, career, community. I use the practices to compete; I use them to grow teams; I use them in my classroom. I also believe that the CENTER principles can lead to growing a great company.[161] In this chapter, I will discuss some particular ways to make the CENTER practices practical in your life.

Here are some of the steps I take in planning my week:

Character. I examine my Life Ring and Courage Mirror daily, in my morning prayer time. I find that I need to re-remind myself every day what my life is about, because the huge number of inputs that come into my mind serve to distract me from what I think is most important. For me, the things that take precedence are my strong faith, my wife and kids, my work at Penn State (teaching courses, chemical engineering research, various service), my ventures with Wild Scholars and CENTER (and soon, "Physics of

Community" research), and our close friends. I love American football, but at this stage of my life, I am not able to follow it as much as I would hope. I love traveling with my family, but at this stage of my life, I cannot do it much. I start from my Character.

Relationships. I look at my list of birthdays and anniversaries – especially for my own family! – and list those for the coming week. With my wife, we determine if we have any plans to see friends or family, or if we want to make plans. We also assess whether there are any "Stones" we need to celebrate, or want to create.

Entrepreneurship and Excellence. I determine the "high point moments" that I want to have that week, and discuss these with my family. I examine my WIG for the semester in light of my Lead and Lag goals, and decide if there is one or two smart experiments I want to run that week.

owNership. Based on my Character, I make my Big Rock choices for the week, and I put them on the calendar. I almost fill my calendar every week, before it starts. Once the week starts, if something needs to change, I change it. But I have the spaces filled. My wife and I plan our week together, usually on Saturday morning. I set my "agents" to work, doing the budget on Saturday morning, and exercise most mornings before I leave the house.

Tenacity. Every morning during my prayer time, I consider the voices coming into my head, to make sure they are the right voices. My Courage Mirror helps me to stay on track, avoiding the croakers

Interview potential hires for their CENTER profile.

Every semester my students go to the Career Fair at Penn State, and they get questions from interviewers. Almost every question fits under CENTER. Here is one list of questions, taken from each of the exercises in this book (by number):

C1. Who were the biggest influences on your life?

C1. What are the 3 most important events of your life?

C2. What 3 things you do now, do you treasure most?

C3. Who are your heroes?

C4. What values did you learn at home?

C5. What 4 ways might you dignify a co-worker?

E1. Have you started any big ventures in the past year?

E2. What limits would you put on pursuing a great idea?

E3. How do you keep track of your ideas, so you don't forget?

E4. What are your 3 biggest failures in life?

E5. What small experiments have you tried, for a hobby?

E6. Do you see any un-tapped resources here at our company?

E7. Talk about a time when your awareness led to serendipity.

E8. Have you ever found yourself in the "right place / right time"?

N1. How will you handle the flood of new stuff from this position?

N2. What are some habits you are glad you have, or wish to change?

N3. How do you schedule your major choices for a week?

N4. Do you run your gas tank dry, or refill at ¼ tank?

N5. How do you make sure that your choices actually happen?

N6. What is your strategy for handling repeated tasks?

T1. How do you handle discoursing remarks?

T2. Say you wanted to lose or gain 20 pounds. How to do it?

T3. How do you handle nay-sayers? Or boredom?

T4. Your division is changing products. What do you do?

T5. How often do you get away for a few days, or a week or two?

E1. What are the last 3 skills you remember purposely learning?

E2. What metrics did you use to build those skills?

E3. Who critiqued you as you grew those skills?

E4. You want to improve your family dinner hour. How to do it?

E5. What are the 3 best books you have read in the past 6 months?
R1. Who are the 5 most important people in the world to you?
R2. Where do you see being "home"? Why?
R3. Are there any manners that especially irk you, when not done?
R4. Give me 2 cases of confrontations, and how you handled them.
R5. What criteria do you have for forming teams?
R6. Are you in a stage where you need autonomy, or power?
R7. What memories do you celebrate each year?

The primary point is not that you must use these particular questions, but rather, that you want to have a mindset of CENTER when interviewing, so that questions more naturally flow. Write down the questions, and learn the whole profile of the candidate.

When I hire a student for my research lab, I always ask that they email me a PDF resume and a link to a 2-minute YouTube they create. I want to see in that brief YouTube video how well they fit the CENTER profile that I need for my position – my "scorecard", as Smart and Street describe in their outstanding book on hiring called *Who*.[162] Every position I hire for is different: Sometimes I need outstanding owNership skills, sometimes strong Entrepreneurship skills, sometimes outstanding Excellence. And most often, I need some combination of all six CENTER practices. For example, if a person has strong skills in Excellence, but they do not see others in the lab with an Eye of Dignity (Character), they likely won't fit into the DV Lab Group.

Up to this point, I have described an interviewer who has a set of questions, which he or she wants to know about a candidate. If you are at a dinner party, you can ask similar CENTER questions, especially if you are shy. In fact, in my own case – and it is quite possibly just because I know my own methods – I can learn more about a person by learning about their CENTER profile, than from knowing their Myers-Briggs type, their DISC personality, or other similar profiles.[163]

Here is an example: "Last year I played on the church softball league. I'm not sure I got 2 hits all year! Have you ever had that happen – just failing really badly at something, after putting a lot of effort into it?" Here you have asked about the person's Failure Resume, and perhaps also about their Scratch List if the event seared into their memory. Here is another example: "I know that my colleagues always wish I were smarter. You know, sometimes I can just hear their voices – do you know what I mean?" You have invited the person to tell you about the voices they hear. In keeping the CENTER categories in mind, you can ask questions that tell you specifically about another person.

Tell interesting stories.

In his book *To Sell is Human*,[164] Daniel Pink talks about the 6-part storytelling procedure of Pixar Animation Studios.

1. *Once upon a time there was ___.* In this step, we learn about the <u>C</u>haracter and <u>R</u>elationships of the characters, and perhaps especially one character. Scenes are played that show the character as funny, clumsy, playful, sad, or other emotion.

2. *Every day ____.* Here a monotony sets in, that must be changed! The character's choices have moved into ow<u>N</u>ership routines that must be changed. <u>R</u>elationships might be lost in this step.

3. *One day ___.* It's a moment of <u>E</u>ntrepreneurship! A risk, an experiment, a serendipity!

4. *Because of that, ____.* The character develops some area of competence or <u>E</u>xcellence, gaining some ground.

5. *Because of THAT, ____.* In many stories, there is a moment when that newly found Excellence will be tested, and the character will have to overcome voices or battles with <u>Tenacity</u>.

6. *Until finally ____.* <u>Excellence</u> shines through, and <u>Relationships</u> are restored!

I think back to my Dad's story in the coal mines. In simplest form, it might read like this:

Once upon a time, Dave was in high school. Every day he would go to school, and then go to the coal mine his father owned to drudge through loading one or two tons of coal. One day, Dave decided to go to West Virginia University to study. Because of that, he happily registered for classes and moved to Morgantown, and life was looking up! But Dave entered a challenging major, Mechanical Engineering, struggled through his first semester, earning only a 1.6 GPA, and had to think to himself, "Is this really what I want to do?" Until finally he decided that he did not want to go back to the coal mine for the rest of his life, and when he studied harder and smarter, he eventually ended up second in his class, and had an outstanding career as an engineer. The end ☺

Strategic planning. Vision-mission-values-strategy.

As I write this book, my department and all the others at Penn State are working to develop our "strategic plan". Our department's plan will go into the College's plan, and the plan from the College of Engineering will go to Old Main, where the administrators will make the final decisions.

The process for writing a strategic plan for a unit usually involves an entire organization or family – and is often met with eye rolling. Most strategic plans suffer from at least one of the following: 1) The plan consists entirely of words, and therefore lacks expression! 2) The plan is written using too many words, so that nobody can remember what it says. 3) The plan is so vague that the document says nothing that is actionable. 4) The "to do" list is so long, that the unit is doomed before they even start.

Strategic plans might seem like they require a lot of effort. But as Stephen Covey describes in the *7 Habits*, every creation really has two creations: a mental creation, and a physical creation. We first design the creation in our minds, and then we execute to achieve the physical creation. We must avoid throwing out this valuable tool, just because it is hard.

Strategic planning usually involves creating at least four key statements to guide self, family, or organization. A *vision statement* is the "preferred future picture".[165] Although the statement is given in just a few words, the picture invariably conjures us detailed meaning for the participants. When I say, "I want a home on the beach," I do not simply mean I want to own a dwelling near to an ocean. I mean I want a getaway in Ocean City, New Jersey, near the boardwalk, where I can talk long walks along the water with the sun rising, get Johnson Popcorn and Manco Pizza, where I can visit the Tabernacle on Sunday ….

A mission statement, sometimes called a purpose statement, provides more about the approach, or the "driving force" that describes how a person, family, or organization will thrive.[166] For companies, a mission statement might be given in terms of the products offered, technology, method of sale, method of distribution, or other driving force.

Values describe the constraints that a person, family, or organization remains within. Procter & Gamble list five primary values on their website – reminiscent of the "Virtuous Hand" described earlier: Leadership, Ownership, Integrity, Passion for Winning, and Trust. Within their PDF document containing these values, they provide more description.[167] Strategy describes the path, or steps, that a company will take toward reaching their vision. Then the whole strategic plan is often evaluated against various acronyms, such as SWOT (strengths / weaknesses / opportunities / threats) or STEEP = social-cultural / technological / economic / ecological / political-legal.

However, a strategic plan must reach more than our mind – the plan must reach our heart and soul and body as well. The steps of CENTER provide a new perspective on strategic planning for your self, family, or organization. By its nature, a large part of a strategic plan represents the Character of a unit, although the strategy often involves the other parts of CENTER.

Your vision statement – your "preferred future picture" – already exists within your Courage Mirror. The Velegol family does not confine ourselves to "10 words or less" for our vision, but instead we *surround* ourselves with our vision statement, who we want to be, with tangible symbols. We have an old family Bible – which we had re-bound for our first Christmas present – to reflect back to us our deep faith, and to remind us where we have been. We have a painting by a local artist that we purchased at our Montessori school's silent auction one year, which reflects back to us how we value using discovery-based education, and hearing the voice of children. We have a photo of blossoms on a *Moringa oleifera* tree – given by a former student – which represent our dedication to using science, research, and engineering to produce food and clean water for people all over the world. We can see our Courage Mirror in seconds, and yet it expresses powerfully our direction in the years or decades to come. Our Courage Mirror is a synecdoche, where each symbol represents many things, and at the same time, the many symbols represent one whole life.

A mission statement can be recast in light of the Life Ring. On one page, in a single diagram, I can highlight 5 to 9 core arenas of my life, and describe how each is contributing to my vision. Some readers might even choose to make a 3-dimensional model of their Life Ring, with more realistic components, in order to symbolize and represent their arenas and methods for reaching their vision. Some might express their Life Ring in terms of a song, with voices and various musical stretches representing their life.

Our values are given by our Virtuous Hand – the 5 primary virtues you will hold – which are represented in the Courage Mirror. In the Velegol home, we use books to convey these virtues, which include for us faithful, experimental, systematic, bold, disciplined, and dignifying – OK, so we have 6 fingers on our hands!

The final piece of a "strategic plan" often falls short in organizations, because there are too many plans. At one meeting for our Department of Chemical Engineering, a representative from DuPont told us that her unit seldom has more than 2 strategic goals at a time. Representatives from Shell and Dow agreed. As one book, the *The 4 Disciplines of Execution*,[168] has described, companies have more than enough plans! What they often lack is a clear plan for execution, and this in part is because they have too many "big goals". When we are pursuing Excellence, either personally or in an organization, we must stake out just one or two major goals, and a system for measuring and keeping account of progress each week, to avoid any confusion about what is the next step.

As an extreme example, what is the vision statement of the United States of America? How could anyone state something so complex in a few words? And yet, when I watch *The West Wing*, and how President Josiah Bartlet and his staff make decisions, the vision is always clear: Many scenes take place in the Oval Office, with a painting of George Washington watching the participants. Other scenes take place with a painting of Abraham Lincoln in the background. George Washington and Abraham Lincoln – as long ago as they lived – make the vision more powerful in my heart than any words that could be written.

What is the "to do" here, in order to write a strategic plan from a CENTER perspective? Simply continue improving the clarity of your Character – Life Ring, Courage Mirror, Hand of Virtue – and make them as expressive as possible, using symbols of art and other representations. Work to keep the symbols fresh, especially for new people, such as children in a family or new staff in an organization, so that they understand the deeply held meaning of the symbols. In defining the path forward, choose not 10 courses of action, but focus on choosing 1 or 2 paths, and upholding accountability for them. These simple steps will lead to a strategic plan that is memorable and powerful.

Embrace synergies, tensions, and feedback.

A theoretical, and yet very practical, part of living is in appreciating the synergies and tensions that exist in various parts of our lives. That is, sometimes our practices cooperate with each other, and other times they compete. Furthermore, sometimes they interact over time, giving feedback between various practices. Here are a few examples of many, which arise out of CENTER:

Character leading to Entrepreneurship. Milton Hershey built the industrial school that eventually became Milton Hershey High School, partly arising from his Scratch List of having a rough childhood, and partly arising from the fact that his wife Kitty and himself couldn't have children. Our deep Scratches – our stories – coupled with how we view those Scratches – our Courage Mirror – frequently lead to our great ventures in Entrepreneurship.

Character improving owNership. The decisions we make in the next hour determine what we actually do. When these decisions are guided by the long-term vision from our Character, it helps the hour-by-hour decisions lead to our greatest ambitions.

owNership leading to Entrepreneurship. Some of the Outstanding Engineering Alumni from our Chemical Engineering Department have built or purchased companies, simply in order to finance broader ambitions. That is, they recognize a need to produce Slack Resources, and they were able to invest these into their Ventures. I think of Jack McWhirter and Bill Joyce as two among many who have done this.

Tenacity helping owNership. I have a note in my journal saying that on 2011 August 27, my FujiScan ScanSnap S1500 scanner stopped working. I had just bought it a couple months before, and so I was quite upset! But my wife Stephanie said, "Own your stuff – don't let your stuff own you!" That little sentence brought me back to my Tenacity senses – hold on toward my Vision, despite all obstacles – and helped me to make a 5 minute phone call, in which a technician helped me to find a tiny pebble lodged in my scanner! We had had some builders doing work in our home, and a small pebble got lodged in the machine. This scanner has been absolutely great ever since. Sometimes Tenacity can get your day-to-day schedule back on track.

Entrepreneurship as offense; Tenacity as defense. Entrepreneurship is about getting started, seeking new Ventures, trying new ideas. It is offense, trying to advance. Tenacity involves protecting your vision, your ideas, your stuff, so that outside forces do not steal them away. Both are needed, as shown in the diagram in the first chapter.

Tenacity sustaining Character or Excellence. Have you ever promised yourself to change your Character, and to gain a particular habit or trait? And then 2 days later you have already failed? Don't give up! Keep setting up the Willpower Tunnel, so that you won't allow yourself to make an easy decision that will trip you up. For instance, if you want to learn to speak Spanish, and you find it hard to study each evening after school or after work, then set up a Willpower Tunnel. Arrange with a friend or colleague to meet at the coffee shop from 8:00-8:45 each evening to practice Spanish together, and if you need it, add that if anyone has to cancel more than once in a given week, that they buy the next 2 cups of coffee.

Entrepreneurship competing with Excellence. Entrepreneurship is about exploring ideas, trying new things, playing. Once we gain some competence at something, and start doing well, we might pursue Excellence so that we can compete. But Excellence can lead us to refine in great detail particular skills we have, such that we stop seeking new Ventures and ideas like we once did. For example, when I started teaching at Penn State, I tried many different strategies for active learning. Many worked OK, and I found a few ideas that tended to work well. After about 8 years of teaching, I started trying to take those few ideas, and really making them Excellent. However, as I did that, I had less time to try new ideas, but I could focus on truly high-impact ideas that significantly enhance the course. This back-and-forth between Entrepreneurship and Excellence is quite common. The key is not to get so far down either path that you lose sight of the other. If you have all Entrepreneurship with no Excellence, it can eventually become like dreams lying in the cemetery. Or, if you have all Excellence and no Entrepreneurship, it can be dry bones with no juice. The balance is necessary, and it is a key tension.

Tenacity helping Relationship. In loving our 3 and 12 or 70, we will inevitably have conflicts. These can even lead to a disintegration of relationships. However, this is where loyalty can be systemized a bit to give Tenacity. We can form a Willpower Tunnel that makes it difficult for a relationship to cease, even amidst storms and chaos. Marriage has done this for centuries, and this institution appears at present to be opening to same-sex couples. Being part of a group, a club, a church, or other institution can help provide the few extra days or weeks of interaction needed for people to work through differences, instead of going their separate ways.

Entrepreneurship-Relationship-Excellence feedback. When we want to start a new idea, we might start as the only one. Entrepreneurship often requires that you step out alone … at first. Soon, however, one might find that a team is required to make the idea move ahead, so that the idea can gain Excellence and make a difference. One you have that team, you will again need to iterate at some point, back to Entrepreneurship, so that you can come up with new ideas to sustain or grow the original idea, or perhaps even the team that launched the idea. Feedback and iterations are very important in CENTER.

Character-owNership-Excellence   trap   …   and Entrepreneurship escape. Sometimes we can block ourselves into thinking that we won't act until we believe strongly in something, and at other times, we won't believe until we have experienced something. Here is something that might seem like a small thing, but it was huge to me. When I was 40 years old, I could hardly swim, and I avoided the deep end of the swimming pool as much as possible. However, my older daughter was starting to love the deep end of the pool, and wanted me to play there with her. I was torn: I wanted to enjoy playing with my daughter in the pool, but I had a fear of the water! I love my daughter, but does that mean that I had to spend time playing with her in the deep end of the pool? It wasn't part of my Character to play in a swimming pool, was it? At the same time, how could it ever be part of my Character, unless I first knew how to swim, and had some competence so that I would not have fear? How could I break that cycle? The answer – as is often the case in life – is to run small 1% experiments. I tried floating in the shallow end of the pool – and it worked! I kept trying small experiments with the water, until finally I found the courage to go to the deep end of the pool. I remember jumping in … and hanging onto the wall for roughly 10 minutes. No kidding. I was terrified. I was watching both my daughters swim around in the deep end like porpoises – by this time, they were both fine in the deep water. And so I told Stephanie, "I'm going to let go, and if anything happens get me, or call the life guard right away." And I let go. And I floated. Then I decided to go under the water for a few seconds, and come back up. It worked. Before I knew it, I was playing in the deep end of the swimming pool for several minutes. It was one of the most liberating things I have ever done. I overcame fear.

At the beginning of this book, I mentioned three villains: fear, lack of focus, and the inability to run experiments. There are others, but these can paralyze our lives. What is your "deep end of the swimming pool"? Do you feel guilty about changing careers? Perhaps you are afraid to commit to a loved one? Or maybe it is, as in my case, a fear of the water, and an inability to try some small steps.

None of us started as completed works. We have to win our victories one at a time. The miracle is that even "ordinary" people can win extraordinary victories. That includes you. I know it is true. Are you ready to work for your dreams? Are you ready to work your way through the CENTER practices, so that you can pursue your passions and purposes? If so, go get it! If not, run your first small experiment today.

References and Notes

[1] Wooden, John and Jay Carty. *Coach Wooden's Pyramid of Success: Building Blocks For a Better Life* (2010). A 1-page summary of the Pyramid of success appears at http://www.coachwooden.com/pyramidpdf.pdf, and a brief biography of Coach Wooden appears at http://en.wikipedia.org/wiki/John_Wooden.

[2] The full version of Aristotle's *Metaphysics* quoted here can be found at http://classics.mit.edu/Aristotle/metaphysics.8.viii.html: "In the case of all things which have several parts and in which the totality is not, as it were, a mere heap, but the whole is something beside the parts, there is a cause."

[3] This scene from *City Slickers* can be found at http://www.youtube.com/watch?v=2k1uOqRb0HU.

[4] Another sometimes helpful categorization – six "S" words – of these practices is that Character asks, "What is **supreme** in your life?" Entrepreneurship asks, "What new **story** are you trying to write?" owNership asks, "What **systems** are you putting in place for your time-energy-money?" Tenacity asks, "Will you have the **stamina** to finish the job?" Excellence asks, "What new **skills** are you focusing to build?" And relationship asks, "Who and where are you ready to **sacrifice** for?"

[5] John Bellanti, a psychologist in State College PA, introduced me to this idea of "giving yourself permission to think …" Sometimes we are afraid to admit our own thoughts to ourselves, even to improve upon them.

[6] Oswald Chambers, in his *My Utmost for His Highest*, writes on August 24, "Have I been asking God to give me money for something I want when there is something I have not paid for? Have I been asking God for liberty while I am withholding it from someone who belongs to me? I have not forgiven someone his trespasses; I have not been kind to him; I have not been living as God's child among my relatives and friends."

[7] MLK Jr. speech in Detroit, June 23, 1963.

[8] Walton, Mary. Woman's Crusade: Alice Paul and the Battle for the Ballot. Palgrave Macmillan (2010). For a brief introduction to Alice Paul, visit the web site for the Alice Paul Institute (http://www.alicepaul.org) and click on the "Alice Paul" tab.

[9] For a brief report about Quaker views on women and their rights, see http://en.wikipedia.org/wiki/Quaker_views_on_women.

[10] NAWSA became the League of Women Voters after 1920, as the 19th Amendment was being ratified by the states. See

http://en.wikipedia.org/wiki/National_American_Woman_Suffrage_Assoc iation and http://en.wikipedia.org/wiki/League_of_Women_Voters.
[11] Susan B. Anthony, along with Elizabeth Cady Stanton, drafted the 19th Amendment. It was brought to Congress in 1878. The Amendment was certified into the United States Constitution on 1920 August 26, which is now celebrated as Women's Equality Day (http://en.wikipedia.org/wiki/Women%27s_Equality_Day). See http://en.wikipedia.org/wiki/Nineteenth_Amendment_to_the_United_State s_Constitution.
[12] *Top Management Strategies*, by Benjamin B. Tregoe and John W. Zimmerman (1983), describes the power of a "driving force" in business. I see that the same principle holds for our self, our family, our career, and our community. We need to identify that primary driving force.
[13] Duhigg, Charles. *The Power of Habit: Why We Do What We Do in Life and Business.* (2012).
[14] We can have several masters, but at some point, those masters will collide, and one will win. If my family drives my decisions at home, and my boss drives my decisions at work, I can bet that there will come an intersection of those worlds, and I will need to choose one. As the Bible says in Matthew 6:24, "No man can serve two masters: for either he will hate the one, and love the other; or else he will hold to the one, and despise the other."
[15] Stone, Douglas; Bruce Patton, Sheila Heen and Roger Fisher. *Difficult Conversations: How to Discuss What Matters Most* (2010). This book provides a lot of outstanding advice on how to handle difficult conversations in which our identity is shaken. Another good book is by Kerry Patterson, Joseph Grenny, Ron McMillan and Al Switzler, *Crucial Conversations. Tools for Talking When Stakes Are High*, 2nd ed (2011).
[16] Many of us at Penn State had an "identity quake" in November 2011, when the Sandusky scandal came to light. The struggle between who we thought we were – Coach Joe Paterno always taught "success with honor" – and the accusations, evidence, and convictions of crimes that occurred right on our own campus, gave a super-quake.

The child sexual abuse that Sandusky was convicted of was absolutely awful. I have two girls, ages 10 and 8, and like most parents, I feel this deeply. And so I personally am still struggling with many parts of the scandal. More will come to light in the trials of 2014. Over the past 2 years, I have learned to wait for evidence in a court of law.

That said, the students at Penn State have overall been amazing. They have had fundraisers, helped awareness, and been champions for both Penn State and for children. Our students are an absolute inspiration, and they are a big reason why "We are ... Penn State!" still has such a powerful meaning here on campus.

[17] Schwarzenegger, Arnold; and Douglas Kent Hall. <u>Arnold: The Education of a Bodybuilder</u>. (1978). The original hardcover has the great bicep shot, with mountains in the background.

[18] I also used to read Schwarzenegger's *Encyclpedia of Modern Bodybuilding* continuously. Not only did the large book have inspiring photos of bodybuilders, and histories, but Arnold outlined a full system for building one's body. I have become an immense believer in systems.

[19] For an introduction to visualization, see http://en.wikipedia.org/wiki/Creative_visualization. For a more "academic look" at imagery or visualization, see Tony Morris, Michael Spittle, Anthony P. Watt, *Imagery in Sport*, 2005.

[20] Goddard's vision inspired him toward space. Read about the "cherry tree dream"   at http://en.wikipedia.org/wiki/Robert_H._Goddard#The_cherry_tree_dream.

[21] "There are croakers in every country, always boding its ruin." – Benjamin Franklin (*Autobiography of Benjamin Franklin*, p 59).

[22] Assaraf, John; and Murray Smith. *The Answer: Grow Any Business, Achieve Financial Freedom, and Live an Extraordinary Life*. Atria Books (2009). Assaraf and Smith define a "vision board", which is type of classic visualization theory. Their book has an important discussion about the "power of the unseen" in shaping our lives. We do not directly control 90% or more of the world around us. For instance, as we drive to work, we trust that the other cars will operate properly, and that the drivers will follow the rules of the road.

[23] Seligman, M.E.P.; S.F. Maier. Journal of Experimental Psychology. **74**, 1-9, (1967). This is perhaps the original paper on learned helplessness.

[24] In Fall 2012, the Velegol family visited the White House. What a Life Ring the President of the United States has around him (and hopefully soon – maybe with my own daughter – her)! As the President weighs major decisions, imagine having the paintings of George Washington, Abraham Lincoln, Theodore Roosevelt, Thomas Jefferson, Ronald Reagan, and others whispering in your ear, "You can do it! You can do it!" It was breathtaking.

[25] Many people are interested in improving the quality of their voice. See for example the book *It's the Way You Say It: Becoming Articulate, Well-spoken, and Clear*, by Carol A. Fleming PhD (2013). This book could be shorter, but it has some useful pointers.

[26] Charles Darwin had a 5-year trip that led to research that changed our lives. http://en.wikipedia.org/wiki/The_Voyage_of_the_Beagle.

[27] See Gladwell, Malcolm. *Blink*, 2005, for his description of the Implicit Association Test and racism. In summary, if we have a racist history, it is likely to stick unless we have new and powerful experiences otherwise. Likewise, see Heath & Heath, *Made to Stick*, 2007, on how Jane Elliott used her "brown eyes / blue eyes" experiment to teach schoolchildren about

racism, after Martin Luther King Jr. was assassinated on April 4, 1968. A summary appears at http://en.wikipedia.org/wiki/Jane_Elliott.

[28] My friend Erik Foley-Defiore looks at a verse or poem or inspirational quote at the beginning of many days, and carries it around all day as an "anchor phrase".

[29] More information about THON can be found at http://en.wikipedia.org/wiki/Penn_State_IFC/Panhellenic_Dance_Maratho n.

[30] In his speech "The Other America" (Grosse Pointe High School - March 14, 1968), the Rev. Martin Luther King, Jr. said
"Cowardice asks the question: is it safe?
Expediency asks the question: is it politic?
Vanity asks the question: is it popular?
But conscience asks the question: is it right? And there comes a time when one must take a position that is neither safe, nor politic, nor popular – but one must take it because it's right."

[31] Anger often results when our expectations are thwarted. Are your expectations robbing your peace?

[32] Craig Bennett, *The Book of Virtues*.

[33] After the Scout Oath or Promise, comes the Scout Law:
A Scout is ... trustworthy, loyal, helpful, friendly, courteous, kind, obedient, cheerful, thrifty, brave, clean, and reverent. See http://www.scouting.org/scoutsource/boyscouts/thebuildingblocksofscouti ng/values.aspx.

[34] Information about Jane Elliott, and her experiment, can be found at http://en.wikipedia.org/wiki/Jane_Elliott.

[35] *Leadership and Self-Deception: Getting out of the Box*. Arbinger Institute (2010). There are earlier editions of this book as well.

[36] Two books that have powerful stories of people passing as others are *Black Like Me*, by John Howard Griffin (1961) and *Nickel and dimed on (not) Getting By in Boom-time America*, by Barbara Ehrenreich (2001). The first has a white man who changed his skin color and passed as black, documenting his experiences. The second book was by a self-proclaimed "myth buster" who took the part of a minimum-wage waitress and documented the experience.

[37] The words from Martin Luther King Jr. in "The Other America" ring loudly about justice and equality. See http://www.gphistorical.org/mlk/mlkspeech/index.htm.

[38] Arbinger Institute, *Leadership and Self-Deception: Getting out of the Box*. (2010).

[39] See http://en.wikiquote.org/wiki/Franklin_D._Roosevelt. FDR gave this line at the Oglethorpe University Commencement Address (1932 May 22).

[40] http://en.wikipedia.org/wiki/Rowland_Hill_%28postal_reformer%29. Rowland Hill had several critical innovations for the postal system.

[41] See http://en.wikipedia.org/wiki/Craig_Venter for a summary of Venter's life, and the Human Genome Project.

[42] See http://en.wikipedia.org/wiki/La_Fille_du_R%C3%A9giment. The nine high C's of "Daughter of the Regiment" are sometimes called "Mount Everest for tenors". The aria's demands move most singers to lower the key by a half or whole step. Pavarotti's performance in 1972 at the Met earned a record 17 curtain calls, and some believe launched his career.

[43] Yunus won the 2006 Nobel Peace Prize for his work. http://en.wikipedia.org/wiki/Muhammad_Yunus.

[44] William Shakespeare, *Measure for Measure*, Act 1 scene 4.

[45] Michael D'Antonio, *Hershey: Milton S. Hershey's Extraordinary Life of Wealth, Empire, and Utopian Dreams*. Simon & Schuster (2007).

[46] Brown, Stuart; Christopher Vaughan. *Play: How it Shapes the Brain, Opens the Imagination, and Invigorates the Soul*. Avery Trade (2010). This book provides a new way of thinking about "play", for self, family, work, and community. Many companies now allow 20% of employee time to "play", within boundaries. Google is perhaps the best known for this, an 3M. But I remember when I was a boy – long before Google existed – that one of my Dad's managers at Weirton Steel said that when he was head of his department, he encouraged his employees to take 1 day per week to try new things, to "play" of sorts.

[47] My friend John Bellanti, a psychologist and life coach in State College PA, taught me how to use this phrase. Sometimes we prevent ourselves from moving forward! That is, we do not give ourselves "permission" to make particular choices.

[48] See http://en.wikipedia.org/wiki/Zone_of_proximal_development for a quick description of the ZPD, and for references to Vygotsky's work. If an experience stretches a person too little, little learning takes place. If an experience stretches a person too much, discouragement sets in, and little learning takes place. The ZPD is the sweet spot where maximum learning occurs, when the person is challenged, but not overwhelmed.

[49] Godin, Seth. *The Dip: A Little Book That Teaches You When to Quit (and When to Stick)*. Penguin Group (2007).

[50] Velegol, Darrell. *Wild Scholars: Designing a learning system for educating Scholars toward their passions and purposes*. (2011). I wrote this book to tell my story about how I see a whole different model of education, which could lead our children toward their passions and purposes. CENTER is part of the book.

[51] The study is given at http://www.asla.org/awards/2006/studentawards/282.html Normally I like studies that have precise controls and clearly defined conclusions. This study, however, intrigues me. I look forward to someone conducting the properly-done experiment, or if it has been done, letting me know about it.

[52] The idea of structure aiding creativity has been examined before. See for instance http://www.forbes.com/sites/stevedenning/2011/03/29/creativity-must-have-structure/.

[53] My wife Stephanie doesn't always like it that I am talking to my recorder! She thinks sometimes I am rude ... and sadly, she is probably correct sometimes. Of course, few things make you look as "cool" as carrying a recorder and talking to it. It is a great fashion symbol!

[54] See Robinson's TED talk at http://www.ted.com/talks/ken_robinson_says_schools_kill_creativity.html

[55] See http://en.wikipedia.org/wiki/Dick_Fosbury.

[56] In *Good to Great*, Jim Collins discusses the importance of the "flywheel effect". This is antithetical to the lottery mentality.

[57] Dungy, Tony; Nathan Whitaker. *The One Year Uncommon Life Daily Challenge.* (2011). See February 22.

[58] See Adapt: Why success always starts with failure, by Tim Harford (2011). Grandiosity can be a killer of ideas! As Harford discusses, a new idea must be "survivable", if the idea does not succeed.

[59] See p 226 of Timothy Ferriss, *The 4-Hour Workweek*, original edition.

[60] Ries, Eric. *The Lean Startup: How Today's Entrepreneurs Use Continuous Innovation to Create Radically Successful Businesses.* (2011). This is an outstanding book that discusses build-measure-learn, and how learning is the #1 job of a startup.

[61] Some people use "plan-do-evaluate-repeat".

[62] Hubbard, Douglas W. *How to Measure Anything: Finding the Value of Intangibles in Business.* (2010).

[63] Michalowicz, Mike. *The Pumpkin Plan: A Simple Strategy to Grow a Remarkable Business in Any Field.* The Penguin Group, New York (2012). Michalowicz discusses three key parts of the pumpkin plan: 1) Start with good seeds, which for large pumpkins can cost $2000 each! 2) Thin down to only the best plants. 3) Nurture those plants like crazy, with water and fertilizer and love. This book is easy to read, and effective.

[64] Sir Ken Robinson's classic TED talk on creativity is found at http://www.ted.com/talks/ken_robinson_says_schools_kill_creativity.html

[65] Conwell, Russell Herman. "Acres of Diamonds". This speech can be found at various places on the internet, including http://www.gutenberg.org/ebooks/368. The speech is featured prominently in Dale Carnegie's *How to Win Friends and Influence People*.

[66] Sivers, Derek. *Anything You Want.* The Domino Project (2011).

[67] Kingdon, John W. *Agendas, Alternatives, and Public Policies.* 2nd edition. Pearson (2010). This book talks about the "garbage can model", and how three items must intersect for change to occur in the political arena: 1) the problem, 2) the solution, 3) the political will.

[68] Duhigg, Charles. *The Power of Habit: Why We Do What We Do, and How to Change.* (2012). He discusses small winds in Chapter 4 on "Keystone habits".

[69] I read a number of books, including Stephen Covey's *7 Habits of Highly Effective People*, and also James A. Autry's *Love and Profit: The Art of Caring Leadership.*

[70] Kingdon, John. *Agendas, Alternatives, and Public Policies.* Updated Edition, with an Epilogue on Health Care. Pearson (2010). I first read this book in 1991, as part of a course with Professor Robert E. DiClerico.

[71] The word "opportunity" comes from the Latin ob portu. Nowadays we have modern harbors, but there was a time when you had to wait for the tide to carry you into the port. If you waited to long, and missed the tide, you had to wait for another day ob portu (for opportunity). Don't let your moment pass.

[72] I love the musical *Mame*, and the song by that title, when Beauregard Jackson Pickett Burnside sings to Mame Dennis, "There's rebel in your manner and your speech ..."

[73] I love the Schumpeter concept of creative destruction, in which a creative idea arises, to destroy an old and less efficient way of doing things. One book, *So What? Who Cares? Why You?* by Wendy Kennedy, describes the importance of placing your new idea along 2 axes, when comparing your new way to an old way of doing things. People are better able to comprehend at this level.

- En. idea. Have a great idea that changes the game, transforming the way people live, and reducing their pain. See 2 axes that others can't, which often takes 15 years to get enough "no's" to identify! Often price-quality-convenience.

- Creative destruction (). - En. Good-fast-cheap (quality-convenience-cost). The three parts of the triangle.

[74] By the end of his life, Richard Price came to think of the American Revolution as the most important event in history, after Christianity. See http://nationalhumanitiescenter.org/pds/makingrev/alltextsthemes.pdf.

[75] One example of how old leaders keep old rules is described in an insightful book called *Why Nations Fail: The Origins of Power, Prosperity and Poverty* by Acemoglu, Daron and Robinson, James A. (2012). During the reign of Tiberius, a man created an unbreakable glass, and went to Tiberius for a reward. Tiberius asked whether anyone else knew about this, and the man responded "no". Tiberius had the man dragged away and killed, so that the idea would die, lest gold become as cheap as lead. The old leadership often wants the status quo.

[76] "owNership is not about what you possess. It is about what you nurture." I heard the owner of a dance company say this prior to a performance of the Nutcracker.

[77] Herb Simon – one of my heroes – studied decision making for almost his entire academic career. He coined the term "satisfice" = satisfy + suffice, because he believed that humans have a limited rationality, due to our finite nature. He wrote several books about bounded rationality and satisficing, starting with *Administrative Behavior* in 1947. Simon won the 1978 Nobel Prize in Economics, and I was able to see him speak while I attended Carnegie Mellon for my PhD.

[78] It is customary for the Cabinet of the United State President to all submit their resignations upon re-election, or election of a new President, so that the President can "re-choose" the Cabinet.

[79] Pastor Jay Passavant of the North Way Christian Community is a wise, knowledgeable, insightful pastor.

[80] http://www.flylady.net/ has organizational tips, calendars, and other methods for maintaining a clean home.

[81] A funny video of Covey working with a learner appears at http://www.youtube.com/watch?v=NoplZCcGVoM.

[82] http://zenhabits.net/simple-living-manifesto-72-ideas-to-simplify-your-life.

[83] I heard Dr. Peter Montminy, a psychologist in State College PA, talk about time. He described 5 steps: 1 awareness of where you are, where you want to be, and where you put your time now. 2 attention to what energizes you. 3 acceptance of your choices (I choose, not I have to). 4 appreciation of the amount of time we have! 168 hours leaves a lot. 5 actions that reflect your values and priorities. I like the way he had us categorize ABC for a listing of many physical-intellectual-emotional-spiritual, then family-community-work. Then he had us sub-prioritize 123 for each of these. Breaking the items down made the consideration of each piece more manageable.

[84] Design is finding and creating alternatives, then choosing among them through evidence-based decisions that lead to determining the best solution for a specific problem. See p 199 of the *Journal of Engineering Education*, April 2012.

[85] My friend Erik Foley-Defiore recommends having meetings in which the participants have the "4 P's": Prepared, punctual, present, positive. Ask your agents for an objective assessment, often by a rubric that you create, comparing to an absolute standard/vision. As President Ronald Reagan often said, "Trust, but verify." George Washington reviewed his troops daily as a general, and he inspected Mt. Vernon each morning by horseback, when he was present. Review frequently.

[86] See Tony Dungy's book, *Quiet Strength*.

[87] Dean Jean Landa Pytel is a firm but very caring assistant dean, who will bend over backwards to help students.

[88] See http://en.wikipedia.org/wiki/SMART_criteria for SMART goals.

[89] See http://en.wikipedia.org/wiki/Frederick_Winslow_Taylor.

[90] See http://en.wikipedia.org/wiki/Jeanne_Calment.

[91] Ury, William. *The Power of a Positive No: Save The Deal Save The Relationship and Still Say No.* (2007). Stephen Covey has a similar principle in his 7 Habits. The idea is even Biblical. The way to sweep out things that you do not want to do, is to fill the space with things that you do want to do.

[92] Gerber, Michael E. *The E-Myth Revisited.* (2009). This to me was the most influential book on systems that I have read. The story of Sarah and her pies spoke directly to me.

[93] Senge, Peter M. The Fifth Discipline: The Art & Practice of The Learning Organization. (2010). The 5th discipline is systems thinking.

[94] The "Nehemiah principle" described by Andy Stanley in his book *Visioneering* says that we need to re-establish the vision or habit every 26 days. This is based on the story of Nehemiah, from the Old Testament of the Bible.

[95] See the "muda" wastes at http://en.wikipedia.org/wiki/Muda_(Japanese_term). Reduce waste in production, championed by Toyota. One of Muda, Muri, Mura.

[96] Duhigg, Charles. *The Power of Habit: Why We Do What We Do in Life and Business.* Random House, New York (2012).

[97] Gawande, Atul. *The Checklist Manifesto: How to Get Things Right.* Metropolitan Books, New York (2009).

[98] This saying was probably originated by some other person, but I remember my Grandma Velegol saying it, and since I could not find a definite other person who said it, I give credit to her ☺

[99] See http://en.m.wikipedia.org/wiki/Ten_Thousand_Men_of_Harvard.

[100] Right before the actual event, on 1776 December 19, Thomas Paine wrote in *Common Sense*: "These are the times that try men's souls; the summer soldier and the sunshine patriot will, in this crisis, shrink from the service of his country; but he that stands it now, deserves the love and thanks of man and woman. Tyranny, like hell, is not easily conquered; yet we have this consolation with us, that the harder the conflict, the more glorious the triumph." What majestic words!

[101] I love this quote:
"Nothing in this world can take the place of persistence. Talent will not; nothing is more common than unsuccessful people with talent. Genius will not; unrewarded genius is almost a proverb. Education will not; the world is full of educated derelicts. Persistence and determination alone are omnipotent. The slogan "press on" has solved and always will solve the problems of the human race". – Calvin Coolidge (American 30th President of the United States, 1872-1933)

[102] See for instance the article by Helen Thomas at

http://www.seattlepi.com/local/opinion/article/Fathers-anguished-thoughts-on-war-1137142.php.
George Herbert Walker Bush wrote this in a letter to his children December 31, 1990 just before the Persian Gulf War.
[103] Brian Cunningham says that to have tenacity in pushing forward, a person needs 1) someone to love them, 2) something to do, and 3) something to do tomorrow morning.
[104] See the notes on Martin Seligman at http://en.wikipedia.org/wiki/Martin_Seligman, or on "positive psychology" at http://en.wikipedia.org/wiki/Positive_psychology, and the references therein. Seligman is the head of the Positive Psychology Center at the University of Pennsylvania (http://www.ppc.sas.upenn.edu).
[105] The US Military does extensive work with resilience training. See https://www.resilience.army.mil/about.html. There is also an outstanding book, *The Resilience Factor: 7 keys to finding your inner strength and overcoming life's hurdles*, by Karen Reivich and Andrew Shatte (2003), which describes the ABC principles.
[106] Reivich, Karen and Andrew Shatte. *The Resilience Factor: 7 Keys to Finding Your Inner Strength and Overcoming Life's Hurdles*. Broadway Books, New York (2002).
[107] I love the description of founding McDonald's by Ray Kroc in his book *Grinding It Out: The Making Of McDonald's* (1992). He had a huge vision for franchising, and he kept at it until the idea succeeded.
[108] For more info on the "point of no return", see http://en.wikipedia.org/wiki/Point_of_no_return. This site provides links to "crossing the Rubicon" and Cortez "burning his ships" so that the soldiers had to fight.
[109] When I was in high school I had weightlifting partners, and we lifted together every evening. The default was that we would "show up", and if someone was going to miss, that person had to phone in.
[110] At the February 2013 game against Michigan, there were 621 survivors. It was an extraordinarily powerful event.
[111] I love the Nike commercial at http://www.youtube.com/watch?v=m-EMOb3ATJ0. Michael Jordan says, "I've missed more than 9000 shots in my career. I've lost almost 300 games. 26 times, I've been trusted to take the game winning shot and missed. I've failed over and over and over again in my life. And that is why I succeed."
[112] To me, the signing of the Declaration of Independence in 1776 is one of the most inspiring historical events in the world. Every signer knew that the United States would be successful ... or that they would hang by their necks.
[113] Heath, Chip and Dan. *Switch: How to Change Things When Change Is Hard.* (2010). This is a nice book on making a change.

[114] The YouTube for "running and reading" by Will Smith appears at http://www.youtube.com/watch?v=-08M7JpLpl4.

[115] My friend Erik Foley-Defiore often talks about "not taking yourself out of the game". It's one thing to have a competitor resist you, but if you quit and take yourself out of the game, that thwarts your chances at victory!

[116] McFarland, Keith. *Bounce: The art of turning tough times into triumph.* (2009).

[117] There are many examples of huge "on the job" shakeups. Nixon and Watergate. Enron. I am at Penn State, and a type of explosion occurred here when the Jerry Sandusky sex scandal was exposed. From watching how the Board of Trustees acted, how the media acted, and others, I have learned that during times of such enormous transitions, it is helpful to learn the facts in the caldron of the courts, rather than in the latest news brief of the minute. Like others, I look forward to some of the court trials of 2014, in order to clarify the truth, so that justice can continue to be done.

[118] Taking the logarithm of these numbers, 100 hours could be called "Level 2", while 1000 hours is Level 3, and 10,000 hours is Level 4.

[119] See http://www.coachwooden.com/index2.html.

[120] Covey's 7 Habits has a funny story about an "animal school", and the story conveys the importance of staying within your areas of strength. And while most self-help books focus on how to improve areas of weakness, I like how the book *Now, Discover Your Strengths* by Marcus Buckingham and Donald O. Clifton (2001) focuses on strengths, not weaknesses.

[121] Pink, Daniel. *Drive: The Surprising Truth About What Motivates Us.* Riverhead Books (2011).

[122] I love some of the quotes at Jimmy John's Gourmet Sandwiches, such as "The 5 Most Important Items That Have To Be In Place If You Want Your Operation To Excel":
* Absolute sense of urgency.
* Perfect Bread* This is the backbone of our brand. Do it right!
* Flawless, fast, accurate execution* No tomato means no tomato.
* Systems & Procedures 100%*
* Same dynamite perfect sandwich every time* This is the reason people come back, not to see you or me!
– Jimmy John

[123] Jane Butler enjoyed learning from Carol Ann Tomlinson. See http://en.wikipedia.org/wiki/Differentiated_instruction.

[124] For an introduction to Canter's assertive discipline, see http://en.wikipedia.org/wiki/Assertive_discipline.

[125] See Bernice McCarthy's work for 4MAT, for instance at http://www.4mat.eu.

[126] I got to see this game on television, as it happened. I remember it like yesterday. See http://en.wikipedia.org/wiki/1987_NBA_Finals. The video of the event can be found on YouTube.

[127] I saw Dr. Bill Banholzer, VP of Research at Dow Chemical, Speak at the University of Pennsylvania for the "Quinn Fest". Dr. John Quinn is my academic grandfather, and I attend this event each year. In his talk, Banholzer spoke about the need to include more "practical", in order to balance the "possible" that academics usually study.

[128] In Chemical Engineering, we often talk about the field of Process Control in terms of feedback and feedforward control. Feedback control measures what has already happened, like a lag metric, and then decides if a change must be made. Feedforward goals predict what will happen, using a model, and so affect a process before a change occurs, like a lead goal.

[129] See Mooney, Carol. *Theories of Childhood: An Introduction to Dewey, Montessori, Erikson, Piaget & Vygotsky*. Redleaf Press, St. Paul, MN (2000) or http://en.wikipedia.org/wiki/Lev_Vygotsky for an introduction to Vygotsky's concept of the zone of proximal development (ZPD).

[130] See http://en.wikipedia.org/wiki/The_Boy_and_the_Filberts.

[131] See http://en.wikipedia.org/wiki/Subterranean_river.

[132] There is an interesting balance between "Entrepreneurship" and critique, and you need to wear these hats at different times. As Richard Zare, the famous chemist at Stanford, once said, "Become a happy, contented schizophrenic, believing and not believing at the same time. If you believe too easily, then you will delude yourself; if you are too critical, you will never try the outlandish. Become your own worst critic but simultaneously dare to try something different."

[133] Pastor Vic King emphasizes this balance between tough and tender. He learned about it while visiting prisons. One book that I have found on this subject is *Compelling People: The Hidden Qualities That Make Us Influential*, by John Neffinger and Matthew Kohut (2013). They call it "strength and warmth".

[134] For examples, see http://en.wikipedia.org/wiki/Problem_solving.

[135] See http://en.wikipedia.org/wiki/Historical_method and the references therein.

[136] See http://www.nytimes.com/1992/12/10/books/books-books-and-more-books-clinton-an-omnivorous-reader.html?pagewanted=all&src=pm for a description of President Clinton's reading habits. In 1982, he read 300 books. Even while he was Governor Clinton and later President, he read significantly. There are many others who read. Nancy Reagan once said about her husband, "He was always reading and writing." My brother Duke once spoke at the Brooke High Graduation, and one of the questions he asked students was, "What books are you reading right now?"

[137] Some of the books I have read on these topics include 1) Mortimer J. Adler and Charles van Doren's *How to Read a Book* (1940), 2) Steve Leveen's *The Little Guide to Your Well-Read Life* (2005) – which I really enjoyed – 3) Kevin H. Kelly's *Books That Shaped Successful People* (1995), and 4) W. John Campbell's *The Book of Great Books* (1997).

[138] Carnegie, Dale. How to Win Friends and Influence People. (1936 original, 1981 revised). This book is on "Velegol's top shelf". See http://en.wikipedia.org/wiki/How_to_Win_Friends_and_Influence_People for a summary.

[139] Roberto Clemente was elected to the Baseball Hall of Fame in 1973, after his death, but before the mandatory five year waiting period after retirement. He is the only current Hall of Famer that has had the 5-year rule waived since the rule was started in 1954.

[140] See http://www.puertorico.com/forums/history/12606-night-happiness-died-roberto-clemente.html for the more complete story.

[141] The football practice scene appears at https://www.youtube.com/watch?v=76nhIfp9gr0.

[142] Grant, Adam M. *Give and Take: A Revolutionary Approach to Success.* (2013). This provocative book discusses ways to get ahead ... but giving giving giving more!

[143] See a great TED talk on vulnerability at http://www.youtube.com/watch?v=iCvmsMzlF7o. The opposite of vulnerability is control. Those in control put people off. How can we put ourselves in a position in which we where we show our vulnerability automatically? As Brene Brown says in this talk, shame is the fear of disconnection. "If others find out about me, they will reject me." Vulnerability is the birthplace of creativity, love. Shame and fear kill it. Blame is a way to discharge pain and discomfort, and happens frequently in today's politics she said.

[144] Pritchett, Bob. *Fire Someone Today: And Other Surprising Tactics for Making Your Business a Success.* (2006). The title makes the book sound quite harsh, but the author notes that if you're not firing someone who should go, you're doing them a dis-service, because you're preventing them from finding their true calling. Furthermore, you're saying, "We don't really care about good work around here.". Whom to fire? Whiners, troublemakers, and redundant workers.

[145] See the May 16 entry of *The One Year Uncommon Life Daily Challenge*, by Tony Dungy and Nathan Whitaker (2011).

[146] Fisher, Roger; William L. Ury and Bruce Patton. *Getting to Yes: Negotiating Agreement Without Giving In.* (1991, 2011).

[147] This team had some amazing people! My co-instructors Jack Matson and Kathryn Jablokow have taught me so much, and been amazing colleagues. John Bellanti is a psychologist and life coach who guided us through many processes. Susan Russell is a professor of theatre at Penn State, who helped us to transform our scripting, our videos ... and ourselves. Kate Miffit guided the sequence of the course and other instructional aspects. Trey Morris and Dan Lucas were unbelievable technical gurus, who worked super hard to get details right. Armend Tahirsylaj was a PhD student in education, who had deep insights and new ideas. Kyle Peck was

an important leader at Penn State who made sure we were watched out for. Numerous others also contributed, including people within the University, the College, and the Department.

[148] Lencioni, Patrick. *The 5 Dysfunctions of a Team. A Leadership Fable.* (2002).

[149] Covey, Stephen M. R. *The Speed of Trust.* The Free Press, New York (2006).

[150] Hirschman, Albert. *Exit, Voice, and Loyalty: Responses to Decline in Firms, Organizations, and States.* Harvard College (1970).

[151] Reichheld, Frederick. *The Loyalty Effect: The Hidden Force Behind Growth, Profits, and Lasting Value.* Harvard Business School Press, Boston (1996).

[152] There is a great book describing the difference between inclusive and extractive: *Why Nations Fail: The Origins of Power, Prosperity, and Poverty*, by Daron Acemoglu and James Robinson (2012). This book shows that the *Guns, Germs, and Steel* (Jared Diamond) is why some nations prosper while some languish. You need look no further than what is the style of the leaders. Inclusive leaders tend to give, while extractive leaders suck every ounce of wealth out of society for their own benefit.

[153] Cain, Susan. *Quiet: The Power of Introverts in a World That Can't Stop Talking.* (2013). This is a great book for introverts, which she says includes one third to one half of all people. In *Quiet Strength: The Faith, the Hope, and the Heart of a Woman Who Changed a Nation*, by Rosa Parks and Gregory J. Reed (1994), Rosa Parks says, "I knew someone had to take the first step. So I made up my mind not to move." Wow..

[154] Two of my favorite books on education are co-authored by Myles Horton, the leader of Highlander Folk School. The first is *Unearthing Seeds of Fire: The Idea of Highlander*, by Frank Adams and Myles Horton (1975). The second is *We Make the Road by Walking: Conversations on Education and Social Change*, by Myles Horton, Paulo Freire, Brenda Bell and John Gaventa (1990). He had amazing self-control and wisdom, and the ability to spread that to others, including Rosa Parks.

[155] *Power and Powerlessness: Quiescence & Rebellion in an Appalachian Valley*, by John Gaventa (1982). Gaventa describes 3 dimensions of power, which include a threat power, a non-issues power, and in the third dimension, a perception of issues power.

[156] Boulding, Kenneth E. *Three Faces of Power.* (1989). Bouldings three faces are threat power, economic power, and integrative (community-type) power. These have some similarity to the Gaventa reference above.

[157] Pfeffer, Jeffrey. *Power. Why some people have it – and others don't.* (2010). This book has what might seem to many to be a "cynical view", but it also has many practical aspects of power.

[158] Sometimes a collection of people have power, which they choose not to use because they prefer more autonomy. When a situation arises that calls for power, they use their "slack power" and rise up. Such a case is described in a classic book by Robert Dahl, *Who Governs*? It describes a social science experiment to understand power in New Haven, CT.

[159] Alinsky, Saul. Rules for Radicals. (1989). Alinsky was a disciple of John L. Lewis, the famous union leader who was my Grandpa Kopson's hero, from his coal-mining days. Alinsky's techniques often do seem radical – I think of his "natural stink bomb" technique, which involved feeding about 100 people black beans before an orchestra concert, in order to make a stand. However, Alinsky's skill in community organizing is legendary.

[160] I remember as a boy seeing an episode of the TV show Dallas, in which Jock Ewing tells his son Bobby, "Nobody gives you power. Real power is something you take!" See http://www.youtube.com/watch?v=dGdfPtW56fo. But over many years and decades and centuries, many leaders have shown that there are different ways to gain and use power, which are much more dignifying that this scene.

[161] In *Good to Great*, Jim Collins discusses 7 principles for building and growing a great company. Let me compare his 7 principles to CENTER.

GOOD to GREAT (Collins)	CENTER
1 Level 5 Leadership: Leaders who are humble, but driven to do what's best for the company.	Character. Great leaders have to know who is their company, and where they are going.
2 First Who, Then What: Get the right people on the bus (and the wrong people off), then figure out where to go (right seats). Finding the right people and trying them out in different positions.	Relationship. Forming teams is about getting the right relationships.
3 Confront the Brutal Facts: The Stockdale paradox - Confront the brutal truth of the situation, yet at the same time, never give up hope.	Excellence. Being Excellent requires that you have a scoreboard, confronting the facts.
4 Hedgehog Concept: Three overlapping circles: What lights your fire ("passion")? What could you be best in the world at ("best at") What makes you money ("driving resource")?	Excellence. Choose one or two WIGs.

5 Culture of Discipline: Rinsing the cottage cheese.	owNership. Maintain strong discipline in choosing, executing, and systemizing.
6 Technology Accelerators: Using technology to accelerate growth, within the three circles of the hedgehog concept.	Entrepreneurship. Take smart risks, and run smart experiments, as fast as possible.
7 The Flywheel: The additive effect of many small initiatives; they act on each other like compound interest.	owNership. Systemize 80%, so that you can innovate on 20%.

CENTER also matches a large part of Stephen Covey, although I think there might be more in terms of running smart experiments (Entrepreneurship) in Covey's book.

[162] Geoff Smart and Randy Street, *Who: The A Method for Hiring.* (2008).
[163] See http://en.wikipedia.org/wiki/Myers-Briggs_Type_Indicator or http://en.wikipedia.org/wiki/DISC_assessment.
[164] Pink, Daniel H. *To Sell Is Human: The Surprising Truth About Moving Others.* (2012).
[165] The "preferred future picture" phrasing comes from my friend John Rodgers, CEO of John Rodgers and Associates, whose company specializes in Dale Carnegie Training.
[166] A nice book detailing a variety of approaches a company can use is *Top Management Strategies*, by Benjamin B. Tregoe and John W. Zimmerman (1983).
[167] http://www.pg.com/translations/pvp_pdf/english_PVP.pdf describes P&G's values in more detail, along with their purpose and principles.
[168] McChesney, Chris; Sean Covey and Jim Huling. *The 4 Disciplines of Execution: Achieving Your Wildly Important Goals.* (2012).

Index

Made in the USA
Lexington, KY
18 July 2014